PRAISE FOR *BRAND ON!*
"WHAT GREAT LEADERS ARE SAYING."

"In his inimitable, down-to-earth, cut-through-the-crap style, Brandon Coleman Jr discloses the secret 'Brand ON!' superpower that can defeat evil inefficiencies, triumph over status quo, and inspire customers and employees alike. From young entrepreneurs to experienced C-suite executives—anyone intent on maximizing their bottom line will benefit from this entertaining, enlightening, and invaluable read."

—CRAIG MURRAY, owner, executive chairman, MOCEAN, LLC

"It takes leadership courage to see and address issues with brand alignment, but trust me—your customers see them before you do. In this book, Brandon Coleman Jr urges leaders to relentlessly seek the truth and drive alignment that will power your business."

—BOB JORDAN, president & CEO, Southwest Airlines Co.

"This exceptionally wise book goes well beyond many other books by inspiring readers to implement the brand-strengthening guidance it offers. *Brand ON!* delivers on its promise."

—LEONARD BERRY, PhD, noted author,
University Distinguished Professor of Marketing,
Mays Business School, Texas A&M University

"From boardrooms to dinners at hushed corner tables, Brandon Coleman Jr's rare ability to cut through the clutter never wavers. He manages to fit his expertise from every conversation and engagement into each page of *Brand ON!* His insight will help you turn ambiguous strategies into a crystal-clear manifesto for success. *Brand ON!* will sit next to my favorites."

—CHRIS PARADYSZ, founder & co-CEO, PMX Marketing Agency

"Most consultants are hesitant to release their hard-earned secrets, but Brandon Coleman Jr openly shares what he has learned over his fifty-year career. He cleverly mixes anecdotes with sage advice to help the reader better comprehend brand alignment . . . a great read!"

—BRAD FREELS, chairman & CEO, Midway

"It's a war of creativity and ideas, so I want Brandon Coleman Jr in my foxhole. *Brand ON!* is a must-read!"

—STUART SANDERS, founder, Sanders Consulting Group

"Brandon Coleman Jr shares his remarkable success growing businesses across a wide range of industries. In *Brand ON!: The Hidden Power of Brand Alignment*, Brandon generously, and in a very captivating manner, shares with the world his time-tested recipe for success."

—DR. STEPHEN W. MCDANIEL, senior professor, regents professor emeritus of marketing, Mays Business School, Texas A&M University

"Brandon Coleman Jr writes the book on marketing that most wouldn't dare. With no agenda other than delivering the absolute truth about what works (and what almost never does) in SMB marketing, Brandon is clearly unafraid to ruffle some feathers. My worry is that those who need to read this book the most, never will. Which is exactly why every business owner should."

—MARSHA MURRAY, owner, chairwoman, Murray Resources

"In *Brand ON!*, Brandon Coleman Jr offers a compelling road map for taking your brand to its highest pinnacle. He shares a wealth of experience and insight that is invaluable to anyone serious about maximizing their potential. His real-world stories, detailed strategies, and actionable advice are powerful counsel."

—MICHAEL C. THOMPSON, founder, Thompson 31Fifty Wines, son of book dedicatee

"Finally, a book on branding that provides a relatable and practical approach for small and medium-sized businesses. Whether you're a startup founder, a small business owner, or a marketing professional, this book offers invaluable insights that can transform the way you think about and execute brand strategy. It's a must-read for anyone aspiring to create a brand that resonates deeply with its audience and stands the test of time."

—ERIC POERSCHKE, owner, chairman, Next Level Thinking

"Brandon Coleman Jr's new book, *Brand ON!*, is a masterclass in understanding and harnessing the power of brand alignment. With an engaging and insightful narrative drawn from more than fifty years of professional experience, Brandon makes the complex world of branding accessible and relatable for everyone. Whether you're a budding entrepreneur, a seasoned professional, or simply someone curious about the impact of brands in our daily lives, this book is an essential read. Brandon's expertise offers a wealth of practical advice and thought-provoking perspectives that empower readers to think critically about the costs of having a brand that is out of alignment. *Brand ON!* is more than just a book; it's a road map to cultivating a powerful, authentic presence in a world where individuals and businesses have so much to gain from aligning their brands."

—DR. NATE SHARP, PhD, dean,
Mays Business School, Texas A&M University

"Brandon Coleman Jr inspires entrepreneurs to access the hidden power of brand alignment in *Brand ON!* Well done."

—DAVE ALPERN, president of 9-time NASCAR champions
Joe Gibbs Racing, author of *Taking the Lead*

"The power of brand alignment shot our growth trajectory through the roof. Brand ON!"

—KRISTIN BRITTAN, founder, owner, Hey Sugar Candy Stores

Brand
ON!

THE HIDDEN POWER OF
BRAND ALIGNMENT

Brand
ON!

TIMELESS WISDOM FOR ENTREPRENEURS

BRANDON COLEMAN JR

AN INC. ⓘ ORIGINAL

An Inc. Original
New York, New York
www.anincoriginal.com

Distributed by Greenleaf Book Group

For ordering information or special discounts for bulk purchases, please contact Greenleaf Book Group at PO Box 91869, Austin, TX 78709, 512.891.6100.

Design and composition by Greenleaf Book Group
Cover design by Greenleaf Book Group

Publisher's Cataloging-in-Publication data is available.

Print ISBN: 978-1-63909-051-8

eBook ISBN: 978-1-63909-053-2

Audiobook ISBN: 978-1-63909-052-5

To offset the number of trees consumed in the printing of our books, Greenleaf donates a portion of the proceeds from each printing to the Arbor Day Foundation. Greenleaf Book Group has replaced over 50,000 trees since 2007.

Printed in the United States of America on acid-free paper

24 25 26 27 28 29 30 31   10 9 8 7 6 5 4 3 2 1

First Edition

To Herbert G. Thompson, marketing professor emeritus at Texas A&M University: Thank you for failing me on my first test, then inspiring, mentoring, and loving me to 50 wonderful years of marketing leadership. I never knew why you called me BrandON, but now I understand. Ninety-five years was simply not enough of you.

CONTENTS

Foreword

Have you ever had the jarring experience of someone you thought you knew acting completely out of character? It can quickly cause you to lose trust in a person and even cause a significant rift in the relationship. But brands do this all the time; they promise their customers one thing, deliver another, and wonder why they struggle to reach new heights.

Now imagine the antithesis of this broken promise: a world where every interaction, every communication, and every experience within a brand are a harmonious echo of a single, powerful idea. This isn't a fantasy; it's the essence of brand alignment and a necessity for any business that desires to reach its full potential. And while the complexity of orchestrating such a transformative concert of customer experiences may sound daunting, renowned brand strategist and business leader Brandon Coleman Jr will make you the maestro of your brand.

Brand ON!

The author's approachable writing style distills over five decades of powerful lessons into an intelligible and coherent narrative. Through engaging real-life stories, Coleman takes you on a journey from confusion to enlightenment, showing you how small adjustments can make significant differences in your brand's performance. And while everyone can benefit from these ideas, this book is exceptionally potent for the small- and medium-sized enterprises who are striving for growth in today's competitive markets.

As you immerse yourself in this game-changing book, you may wonder if teachings on brand alignment garnered over the last 50 years can weather the shifting tides of today's consumer preferences. I can say, with absolute certainty, that the lessons contained in these pages are more relevant than ever before. In fact, I would posit the rise of millennials and Gen Z have made *Brand ON!* a must-read for any leader attempting to navigate today's markets. These younger consumers are not just seeking products or services; they are on a quest for meaningful experiences. They demand authenticity and alignment in exchange for their trust and loyalty. They yearn to support local businesses but expect the same level of professionalism and polish they encounter with big brands and big budgets. Fortunately, this book gives you the tools to address this new paradigm and to bridge the gaps between the consumer's desire for local support and the necessity of delivering a consistent brand experience.

I was fortunate enough to have these teachings bestowed upon me at a young age but took them for granted with the glib assumption that every teenage boy was given this type of elite brand leadership training. It was only after I achieved career success as an executive at several large companies that I realized both the importance of brand alignment and the rarity of its occurrence. Thankfully, my father, the author of this book, was patient enough to wait 20 years for me to say, "Wow! You were right."

Absorb the information, enjoy the journey, and transform your businesses by turning your Brand ON!

—BRANDON C. COLEMAN III
CEO, president, and CMO to multibillion-dollar brands
son and student of a brilliant father and brand maestro

Acknowledgments

I would like to express my deepest gratitude to the following people:

The hundreds of clients who have allowed me to dive into every part of their business and many times, personal lives, in order to bring them into more perfect brand alignment,

The thousands of executives who have shared their wins, and more importantly, their losses,

The millions of consumers who have responded to my clients' brands,

My brother Kevin, whose talents as our creative director hypnotized clients long enough for them to buy into my counsel,

My covenant friend Bill Peel, a brilliant visionary who can change the world on a whiteboard,

My right arm and confidant, Debbie Kasper, who is not only a talented media buyer but a dear lifelong friend,

Brand ON!

Eric Poerschke, my former EVP, inner voice of wisdom, brand consulting guru, and good friend,

Kirk Loudon, our co-creative who is an amazing talent and a good friend,

Stuart Sanders, a great friend and confidant whose 25 years of business and life guidance was invaluable, in memoriam,

Texas A&M University, its' core values, discipline, Mays Business School, and The Aggie Network,

The Mays Business School Marketing Department and its many outstanding professors who have been lifelong friends and counselors,

Dr. Rajan Varadarajan, who has the dubious honor of sitting in the Brandon C. Coleman Jr Chair in Marketing,

Dr. Dan Baker, PhD, creator of the Canyon Ranch Health & Wellness Center in Tucson, as well as renowned author and friend of 35 years, in memoriam,

The Reverend Dr. Jim Jackson Jr., CEO, author, minister, counselor, 30-year covenant friend and literally the most genuine man I have ever known,

All who by reading this book will give my insights and words a chance to make a difference in their businesses and personal lives,

All of my real friends, who know who they are,

My amazing wife, Carri, who is the epitome of a beautiful woman and wife,

My three accomplished children, who have provided me the immense joys and humility of fatherhood,

My three children's spouses, who put up with me,

Our four grandsons, who I humbly note, are the best four kids in the world,

Acknowledgments

And to the five generations of Brandons in our family.

––––––––––

I would also like to share appreciation with a few people who helped in the actual production of the book:

Linda Baker

Luken Baker

Justin Branch

Erin Brown

Brandon Coleman III

Kevin Coleman

Gwen Cunningham

Dania Demirci

Jen Glynn

Neil Gonzalez

Tanya Hall

Holt Haynsworth

Max Lufer

Marissa McGarah

Madelyn Myers

Gary Peto

William Peel

Kristine Peyre-Ferry

Jeff Ross

Sean Richards

David Russell

Michael Thompson

Nathan True

Benjamin White

Introduction

Chances are, your brand is out of alignment. Most brands are. It doesn't mean your business isn't successful, but if your brand is out of alignment, you can be certain you are not maximizing your potential. Simply put, if your brand is not in alignment, you are leaving money on the table and may not even know it.

Perhaps you don't know what *brand alignment* is. Most people don't. My purpose in writing this book is to bring awareness to the hidden power of brand alignment and the massive impact it can have on your business. I will share the basic fundamentals of a well-aligned brand, expose the major causes of a brand out of alignment, and provide you a checklist of areas you may want to start reviewing to begin assessing your own brand. You will come to understand why brand alignment is not a fad but an invaluable, time-tested way of optimizing the success of your business.

As the consultant to hundreds of clients and a customer to countless more, I've seen far too many independent businesses struggling to reach their full potential—and some even going out of business—due to a misaligned brand. When a brand consultant is on the outside looking in and knows what to look for, the misalignments are blatantly obvious. When an entrepreneur is on the inside looking out, they may never see them. My intention here is to share five decades of awareness and ideas that I hope will shine a light on your current opportunities and provide you some big takeaways to help you reach your ultimate potential.

Brand alignment is an overlooked strategic area in many businesses, which is why it has so much hidden power. You may be rolling along making good money and not even know that your brand is out of alignment and your business is failing to achieve 100% of its potential upside. What if misalignment has crept in and an adjustment or two could provide a 20% increase to your bottom line? That would be a significant improvement. But what if your alignment initiative improved your business by 50%? Moreover, what if you could get your brand in perfect alignment and hit 100% of your potential? That is when the numbers extrapolate, because a business whose brand is in 100% alignment soars in value. That is *Brand ON!*

This book is for the entrepreneurs, small business owners, equity investors, family business leaders, and marketing professionals who want to find their hidden opportunities and amplify their success. It is for the business street fighters and courageous leaders who are willing to immerse themselves into their brand to better understand how all of the little things will make the biggest difference. It is for the majority of US companies, the 33 million-plus small businesses that drive America. Whether you run a brick-and-mortar store, a professional service firm, a nonprofit, a restaurant, a physician's practice, or a development company or whether you make a living as an online influencer, you will find immense value in these pages.

My purpose in writing this book is to bring awareness to the hidden power of brand alignment and the massive impact it can have on your business.

It is not written for the Fortune 500 world, as most small businesses cannot relate to their success metrics, or for the various brand alignment issues they face. While many of their challenges are relevant, that is for another audience at another time. It is not for the faint of heart or those who wear their feelings on their sleeves. It is not for business victims or for those afraid of change. Most importantly, it is not intended for people who prefer to dodge the truth in favor of shooting the messenger. It is for those who want to cut through the clutter and obtain candid clarity with conviction. It is for those who want to leverage the hidden power of brand alignment.

Brand ON! is not for those seeking to read a business literary classic, nor is it written to impress scholarly academics. It is not scribed by professional ghostwriters and is most certainly not a testament to the fine quality of English teachers I had throughout my school years, so don't blame them. If you do find a typo or error, you could do us all a favor by reporting it on the book's website so we can make an immediate online correction for our digital readers. Finally, know for certain this book is 100% human-created content, as AI was not used in its writing. However, you can be sure AI will be reading this book to learn more about brand alignment.

I have seen brand alignment change lives by advancing personal dreams through business improvement. Included as testimony are real-life, small business client stories that will serve as examples and inspiration to my claim. It is my desire to bring the awareness, fundamentals, and power of brand alignment to entrepreneurs and organizations who may or may not be able to afford the services of the very best brand advisors. It's my passion! I love it when a business's brand makes sense. It excites me when an organization exceeds my expectations. It could be something as simple as my morning coffee at the small bistro who totally gets it or a complex B2B consulting engagement preparing to change an industry, but it's truly awesome when a brand overdelivers on its promise. It's also very rare.

My business life began at six years of age, selling snow cones and lemonade and holding carnivals in my backyard for neighborhood friends. It progressed to starting two small businesses while I was in college, one manufacturing collegiate-branded fishing lures and the other selling creative T-shirts. Before I graduated, I was generating marketing and advertising programs for local businesses, ultimately leading me on a journey to creating and counseling hundreds of brands in most every industry imaginable for the next 50 years.

At twenty-four years of age, I founded, developed, and (twenty years later) sold a strategic marketing firm considered by many to be a pioneer in the brand consulting space, long before the Deloittes and McKinseys had entered the fray. I later started a brand alignment consultancy, served on numerous boards, received some awards, and was named an Outstanding Alumnus by my university's business school, where I also served on the Dean's Advisory Board for 25 years. More importantly, I have experienced many business and life failures throughout my journey, which have provided lasting value to my clients and mentees and which, hopefully, will provide similar value to you as well.

During that time, I generated the notes that served as the foundation of this book, capturing the essence of the challenges, victories, and defeats of many different organizations, leaders, families, and entrepreneurs. I will share some of their stories and endeavor to make you aware of the power of brand alignment and communicate its complexities in the simplest form possible.

It is important to note right up front that brand alignment is timeless. What you will discover in these pages is as relevant today as it was with my first client 50 years ago. Sure, the tools, processes, and messaging evolve daily, but the art and science of brand alignment is an excruciatingly nuanced concept that has not changed one bit in five decades. Customer expectations and engagement change, but the need to align your brand for success does not.

Brand alignment is timeless.

While you will not be reading this work to learn all of the detailed intricacies and applications of branding, you will be gaining an astute awareness of the fundamentals of brand alignment, which will enable you to make an immediate positive impact on your business.

If you want to maximize your potential, this book will help you do just that once you apply your newly found knowledge to every aspect of your brand. As you do so, note that marketing and branding strategies always include disclaimers, so you might find a few unique exceptions to what I write, but there won't be many.

We will not spend much time addressing the tools or tactics of branding, such as preferred media strategies, social media trends, artificial intelligence, design styles, planning analytics, content development, SEO, research metrics, creative approaches, performance dashboards, event management, or myriads of other planning, activation, and measurement choices at your disposal. Counsel on which mix and application of these is best for your specific business change constantly as they fluctuate with marketplace dynamics and unexpected disruptions. However, you can be sure none of them will ever reach their full potential without proper brand alignment fundamentals because brand and commerce are so inextricably intertwined.

Brand and commerce are inextricably intertwined.

You will enjoy being able to read this book in short order and immediately benefit from your newly acquired insights. I will take you from fog to clarity and share what it's like to experience aligned brands. I will expose the deepest potholes that destroy brand alignment and challenge you with questions about your own brand.

Please don't put the book down too early when you think it's going to keep relentlessly pounding on you. I will enthusiastically get you on the road to total success and promise to instill hope and opportunity in your future. I'll address your most pressing questions and maybe even make you laugh a little along the way. My sincere desire is to make an immediate positive impact on your business and your life by helping you identify the hidden power of brand alignment as you begin to turn your *Brand ON!*

CHAPTER 1

What Is Brand Alignment?

D on't beat yourself up if you don't know what brand alignment is! The majority of business professionals don't know what it is either. Nor do many of the college marketing professors and business school department heads I recently visited. The truth is, not enough marketing agency professionals are as up to speed on it as they should be. So why is it so evasive, so hidden? How can something I believe is arguably the most valuable asset in your business arsenal be so hard to see? To better understand brand alignment, allow me to start by sharing my definition of *brand*.

WHAT IS A BRAND?

There are a plethora of definitions and perceptions of *brand*. My favorite, which our firm created and used since 1980, reads, "A brand is a promise wrapped in a delivery." I like what it stands for and how it simply states that your business makes a promise and backs it up by delivering on that promise. Even though scores of branding firms and definitions have come and gone in the last five decades, this is still my favorite.

A brand is a promise wrapped in a delivery.

Google the definition of brand today, and you will get something like, "A brand is a product, service, or concept that is publicly distinguished from other products, services, or concepts so that it can be easily communicated and usually marketed. Branding is the process of creating and disseminating the brand name, its qualities, and its personality." While technically correct, what does that mean, and how does it affect your business? I have found, when counseling clients on anything brand, that simpler is better. Great brands are simple.

Seeing as how I have always held a special place in my heart for the cowboys of the American West, I like their definition of brand: "An identifying mark burned on livestock or criminals with a branding iron." Yeehaw!

A VERY BRIEF HISTORY OF BRAND

The basic premise of *brand* has been around for a very long time. It was thought to have started in approximately 2000 BC, when farmers used it to identify their properties and craftsmen put their mark or symbol on goods to label them as their own. Even though it was used to a degree to market products by some of the major New York and Chicago ad agencies in the post–WWII era of the 1950s and '60s, the strategy of branding as a master discipline really began gaining momentum with the corporate marketing world in the 1980s.

When I graduated from college with a business marketing degree in 1978, the word *brand* was seldomly discussed in the classroom and rarely used to talk about anything other than a logo or a mark, similar to how it had been for thousands of years. By the time I sold my first brand strategy firm in 2000, business schools were finally beginning to talk about it in a meaningful way. From the 2000s on, the modern era of branding took off, and we witnessed an explosion with the expansion of the internet, an increase in students majoring in marketing, extensive job growth in marketing-related fields, and a surge in brand terminology. In fact, the rapid explosion of *brand* ultimately gave birth to the branding nomenclature overload we experience today.

> Brand. Branding. Brand activation. Brand agency. Brand ambassador. Brand archetype. Brand architecture. Brand assets. Brand attributes. Brand audit. Brand awareness. Brand beliefs. Brand delivery. Brand dilution. Brand discovery. Brand equity. Brand experience. Brand extension. Brand gap. Brand guidelines.

Brand harmonization. Brand hierarchy. Brand identity. Brand image. Brand integrity. Brand intention. Brand management. Brand logo. Brand mark. Brand map. Brand mission. Brand personality. Brand perception. Brand personas. Brand pillars. Brand positioning. Brand preference. Brand promise. Brand purpose. Brand salience. Brand standards. Brand story. Brand strategy. Brand valuation. Brand values. Brand vision. Brand voice. Cobranding. Generic Brand. Master Brand. Off Brand. On Brand. Parent Brand. Rebrand. Service brand. Subbrand. And so on.

Quite a list, isn't it? Do you think all of the marketing execs running around town are in agreement with the definition of those terms, much less the alignment and execution of each as it relates to your business? Consulting firms are having a heyday selling the articulation and activation of this confusing verbiage. Counseling totally confusing clients has become a profitable art, because leaders are willing to pay for clarity. As an entrepreneur, you just want to know what's most important. You want to know what you can do today to improve performance.

WHAT IS BRAND ALIGNMENT?

Brand alignment is the sum of all of the nomenclature listed earlier perfectly executed.

I'm kidding. Only a few sporadic definitions of brand alignment actually exist, because it is such a misunderstood concept. The proliferation of brand nomenclature only adds to leaders' confusion regarding the matter. The good news is you don't have to master every brand term to achieve brand alignment. In fact, if you start with a simple definition of brand alignment and a relentless focus on its execution, you will find that every brand practice listed earlier will come together in harmonious fashion to help your business reach its full potential, to be Brand ON!

My definition of brand alignment is short and simple: "Brand alignment occurs when the customer experience meets customer expectations," or CX = CEXP. Brand alignment is the magical moment when every single touchpoint of your brand represents and delivers what your customers want your brand experience to be. Once you are aligned, the strength of your organization's brand alignment is perpetuated by how well you and your employees understand, communicate, and consistently deliver on your brand's promise, key attributes, metrics, and messages.

Brand alignment occurs when the customer experience meets customer expectations.

Let's be really clear about one very important fact: Brand alignment is much more than marketing. Marketing is certainly one of the primary variables included in the brand alignment mix, but marketing is not the sole driver behind alignment, nor is it the only discipline necessary to lead an alignment initiative. Simply put, branding is who you are, and marketing encompasses the tactics

you will use to build awareness of your brand. All of your marketing initiatives will become much more effective once your brand
is in alignment.

Brand alignment is much more than marketing.

In the late '90s, Jennifer Aaker was credited with defining a
certain set of human characteristics she associated with brands as
a *brand personality model.* Published in the *Journal of Marketing
Research*, she revealed five robust dimensions, similar to the Big 5
human personality scale, where she proved consumers with certain
personality traits are drawn to brands with similar personality traits.[1]
Her brand personality dimensions model includes sincerity, excitement, competence, sophistication, and ruggedness.

Relating to brand alignment, if you chose to build your company on the dimension of excitement, you should not be saying or
doing anything boring. You need to be seen as imaginative, modern,
inspiring, edgy, and spirited. Likewise, if you are in the medical field
and chose to build your brand on the dimension of competence,
then you probably don't want to integrate too much humor into
your patient communications. Competence exudes reliability, intelligence, responsibility, efficiency, and effectiveness. While there has

---

1   Jennifer L. Aaker, "Dimensions of Brand Personality," *Journal of Marketing Research* 34
(August 1997): 347–356.

been much discussion and expansion of Aaker's model, my basic salient point is fairly simple: Everything you do with your brand needs to align with the type of customer, client, donor, or patient you desire to serve.

Everything you do with your brand needs to align with the type of customer, client, donor, or patient you desire to serve.

ART, SCIENCE, OR COMMON SENSE?

Successful brand alignment is a combination of art and science, with a major infusion of common sense. But if I could use only one of the three to create or revitalize a brand, I would choose common sense every single time.

Common sense is at the core of every great brand. Each physical, visual, audible, mental, and spiritual connection with your customer from the very first moment they ever encounter your brand needs to make immediate sense—common sense. If it doesn't make common sense to your customer, then it doesn't work. You can't explain it away. Customers don't have the time or tolerance for you to explain your brand. If any part of your brand—product, service, naming, packaging, marketing, advertising, social, etc.—does not make immediate sense, it creates a friction point, and you will not maximize your ultimate potential. It needs to make sense, it needs to be natural, and it needs to easily flow without excuses. As my High School Hall of Fame basketball coach father put it to his players, "You can give me a win, or you can give me excuses. I don't want your excuses." He won a lot. You don't have time to explain your brand, and your customers won't tolerate your excuses.

Effective brand alignment is when your organization's execution is played out at every discernible touchpoint to ensure your stakeholders' interactions are consistent with the brand's vision, identity, and values. A customer, client, or patient who sees any element of the brand should believe the company delivers in alignment with its promise and that all messages and actions are authentic to their personal journey. Art, science, and common sense: Great brand alignment is all three.

You don't have time to explain your brand, and your customers won't tolerate your excuses.

As a relatable example, think of a dating experience in your past. Your date had done their homework and garnered all the information they could about you from your friends before they asked you out. They learned you were the sophisticated type who loved sashimi dinners, the smooth jazz of Miles Davis, and reading a good book on the weekends. When you first talked, they appeared to be in alignment with those things you favored. When they showed up at the door for that first date, they were certainly dressed to fit your style.

They took you to one of the best sushi houses and had Miles Davis playing in the car along the way. It was a perfect evening, and you were thinking *This is the one I've always dreamed about.* This is an example of brand alignment; everything aligned to the sophisticated personality type you preferred.

After a few dates, those similar passions began evaporating. This person's brand alignment was not authentic, and they began revealing the true nature of their brand. You learned they really didn't like jazz music at all and would not be caught dead reading a book on the weekends. They preferred fried catfish, and their daily attire was really more in line with a monster truck rally than a refined evening on the town. Their real essence continued to show, and your doubt level was on the rise. Your trust deteriorated to the point that you realized this might be a nice person who was trying really hard, but they did not align with their brand promise. They were not in brand alignment, so ultimately, you decided to move on to another brand.

Consumer relationships with your brand are no different. They demand that everything makes sense. From promise to delivery, they prefer transparency, authenticity, and commonality. They want their customer experience with your brand to be frictionless and to never let them down. When it does, they want you to respond in a way that brings your brand back into alignment with their expectations. They don't want excuses; they want wins.

WHAT IS BRAND ON! ACCLAIMED?

Brand ON! Acclaimed is when an enterprise achieves perfect brand alignment, and their customer experience exceeds their customer's expectations, or CX > CEXP. It is when an organization goes above and beyond to overdeliver to their customers, transcending all expectations. Brand ON! Acclaimed is reached when a company's culture embraces an attitude of surprise and delight instead of solely delivering at the level of expectation.

CX > CEXP

Brand ON! Acclaimed is a celebratory exclamation of a business or nonprofit who has taken the time to genuinely understand their audience's expectations and orchestrated a way to consistently overdeliver the value of their brand. Are they perfect every time? Of course not, but when striving for perfect alignment, occasionally falling a little short is acceptable.

I am not suggesting the strategy of underpromising and overdelivering, because that approach risks communicating a lack of confidence or competency in your organization. Overdelivery is also not a good idea as a last-ditch, Hail Mary effort for a failing company. You need to be genuine in putting forth the extra effort and delivering that little surprise without looking like you are trying too hard. It needs to be an authentic integration of gratitude and appreciation into your core values and beliefs.

More often than not, Brand ON! Acclaimed entities have engineered an operating model and supporting business system that enables them to perform at their very best, day in and day out. They have recruited, trained, and inspired team members who care about their customer outcomes. Last but not least, they have created an authentic and transparent brand while curating all of the inspiring visuals, messaging, and content that go with communicating that brand's purpose for being.

Brand ON! Acclaimed is when an enterprise achieves perfect brand alignment, and their customer experience exceeds their customer's expectations.

On brand and *off brand* are terms used in the marketing world to identify how various tactics relate to a brand's image. Brand ON!, if you will, is the ultimate pinnacle of everything coming together for good. So why be Brand ON!? Because it puts your business in an elite group with very little competition, and on top of that, it's fun!

CHAPTER 2

Experiencing Aligned Brands

There is truly no greater consumer joy than experiencing an aligned brand. Think of your very favorite personal buying experiences. What is your go-to brand for your hobby or other passion? Name your most-frequented restaurant that knocks the entire dining experience out of the park every single time. Which clothing line do you totally trust to make you look and feel your best? What is your favorite hotel chain that treats you like you own the place? What business service company consistently exceeds your expectations? You may be able to list a few, but they are the exception.

These exceptional businesses have aligned their performance with their brands and created the culture to support it. They promise a certain level of service, and they relentlessly keep that promise. They intentionally set certain expectations with you and their other customers, and they meet your expectations. For the most exceptionally aligned brands, they exceed those expectations on a regular basis.

WHY ALIGNED BRANDS ARE RARE

We enjoy aligned brands because they are a rarity. When we encounter one, it creates a special feeling of oneness and appreciation, almost like the brand was crafted and delivered just for us. An aligned brand usually brings its emotions and vulnerability to the forefront to create a sense of genuineness and authenticity. Aligned brands are not driven by algorithms, are very challenging to create, and are nearly impossible to duplicate. Aligned brands find the right balance among art, science, and common sense.

Aligned brands are few and far between because they demand great leadership and vision. Truly aligned brands do not come from the bottom up; rather, they align from the top down and are usually orchestrated by a single leader. That leader must have the courage and willingness to assess, own, and address the realities of the organization. They must be willing to see and speak truth, even when it hurts. Too often, simple arrogance gets in the way for many leaders and prevents them from being able to guide an effective brand alignment. The leader must be willing to deal from a place of truth and must desire a keen understanding of the infinitesimal nuances of their brand to bring it all together for success.

Creating and activating aligned brands also requires superior vision and street-sense awareness, so it also helps when that leader has the special ability to see everything at once. Although rare, this "situational awareness" allows them to envision, create, and lead the deployment of the perfect customer experience. The Endsley model, as published in the *Human Factors Journal*, defines *situational awareness* as the perception of the elements in the environment within a volume of time and space, the comprehension of their meaning, and the projection of their status in the near future.[2] That means you possess the unique ability to simultaneously perceive, understand, and effectively navigate your situation while it is occurring. It involves comprehending a given circumstance, gathering relevant information, analyzing it, and making informed decisions to successfully address any potential risks, hazards, or events that might occur. And fast. You don't always have a few months or years to get your business house in order.

Aligned brands are few and far between because they demand great leadership and vision.

The experts will tell you this rare adeptness is what makes for great fighter pilots, race car drivers, quarterbacks, point guards in basketball, and top law enforcement officers. These people can see a whole field of objects without looking. They sense everything

---

2 Mica R. Endsley, "Toward a Theory of Situation Awareness in Dynamic Systems," *Human Factors Journal* 37 (March 1995): 32–64.

around them at once as their minds shuffle through ways the current situation might play out at speed. Patrick Mahomes, the Super Bowl winning QB for the Kansas City Chiefs has it. Basketball great Michael Jordan has it. Racing legend Jeff Gordon has it. Select prominent business leaders have it. You probably know someone who has it and can tell they are simply different. You can try to teach it, create awareness for it, and train for it, which may well yield some enhanced abilities, but there is nothing that matches up with having the actual gift.

Relating to your business, it would be a genuine advantage if you were that rare leader who had the ability to see all of your customers', clients', or patients' journeys at speed. What do they want or need? What will they buy? How much will they pay for it? How will they find you? How will you find them? How will the two of you initially engage? Some of you entrepreneurs inherently have this ability, and some of you do not and will need to find that leader or counsel to help you accomplish your brand alignment. Either way, know that strong leadership and vision are the primary resources you need for success in a brand alignment initiative.

The second primary reason aligned brands are rare is they also require the cooperation and alignment of all of your organization's key business disciplines. Strong leaders of larger enterprises know to focus on the power of alignment within the organization—basically, getting everyone aligned and rowing in the same direction. Finance, engineering, R&D, human resources, IT, marketing, accounting, operations, and all other facets of your organization must be singing out of the same hymnal for optimum performance. That said, the majority don't stop to think about the same concept as it relates to brand alignment.

Busy lining up all of the larger internal organizational functions, the infinitesimal details of the true customer experience slip by. Whether leaders like it or not, customers can literally sense when you are out of alignment; the words and actions they see and hear don't match. What you promise and what they actually see you deliver must match as often as possible. At best, being out of alignment feels inauthentic; at worst, it feels untruthful and dishonest. It is one of the things customers will forgive the least. Great alignment coupled with authenticity is a truly powerful combination.

This same concept holds true in a small to medium business. In fact, it is far easier in a small business, because there are a whole lot less people to bring into alignment. For example, in a microbusiness, it may mean simply getting your one other employee in line with your vision and direction, but it is still critical. Regardless of your size, business alignment must support brand alignment. Many business leaders spend years developing their business model in search of the perfectly aligned customer experience. Through trial, error, teamwork, and consultants, they often embark upon a course of continual improvement in search of this magical delivery. Some of them find it, but many of them never get there. At the end of the day, aligned brands require a special touch, whether created overnight or over time, and they require the support of all the business disciplines. Everyone must be fully engaged, because a brand is only as strong as its weakest link.

Growth can rapidly dilute an aligned brand and is the third reason they are so rare. Frequently, a founder has a clear vision, but as they start to expand the business, they dilute the singularity that made them great. This often comes from outside influences (consultants, board members, etc.) who are seen as "professionals" in their field but who don't fully understand brand alignment prior to making recommendations. It can also come from a creative founder reaching for incremental sales opportunities, which causes them to overextend and lose touch with their original audiences. Finally, it can come from the addition of new team members who do not understand the purpose of the brand and have expanded beyond the daily reach of the founder. Growth is one of the most frequent origins of a misaligned brand, and business leaders are often too distracted by other initiatives to see it.

WHERE PERCEPTION MEETS REALITY

Let's get something straight: It's your job to understand and manage your customers' expectations. If you think your customers expect too much, perhaps you are in the wrong business. Or maybe you have not done a good job of creating the proper expectations to align with your offering. At the end of the day, you are responsible for both the perception and the reality.

To match perception with reality, you first need to know your market. Remember that *everyone* is not a good definition of your customer base; you need to make certain your target market is well defined. In a time flush with data, gathering all key metrics from your prospective marketplace is paramount and not that difficult with today's rich information tools. You need to know where your markets' perceptions are coming from and what generates their expectations for your brand. Depending on your unique industry and current business situation, psychographics, demographics, chronographics, firmographics, technographics, and quantitative and qualitative analysis are all statistical references at your disposal which can give you tremendous insights on your customers' expectations. AI is already compiling this critical information at light speed. Once you have collected that information and have a clearly defined understanding of your market, it will be easier for you to begin identifying your customers' expectations and aligning their perception with reality. But this is just a starting point.

Reality also misses perception if your ads or your social media are sending out messages you can't deliver on. Your choice of words, colors, creative approach, and content attitude could all be sending you off in the wrong direction. Maybe your name conveys the wrong message from the start. It could mean something to you personally but nothing to the marketplace. If a brand is "a promise wrapped in a delivery," what might your wrapper look like? Does it establish the desired initial impression for your organization? Does it give you a chance to match the perception to the reality? If your name is Cheap-o's, it doesn't make sense to be selling luxury goods. If you promise great service, like a "fresh salmon processing service" I recently used in the Pacific Northwest, it doesn't make sense to include in your materials, "All processed fresh-caught salmon will be delivered in 12 to 16 weeks." Fresh? Really? What do they think my perception is when I read that on their order blank? I wish I had kept a 50-year list of the idiotic brand claims I have witnessed.

As business creators and owners, we sometimes think our clients are just out of touch. We think they expect too much service or don't understand how we work. Our pride will occasionally—or frequently, for some—stand in the way of us properly aligning perception and reality. It is usually the small things we don't see that make the biggest difference. Lining up reality with perception is not easy. You have to be able to assess customer interactions with your brand from every possible angle to accurately determine their perceptions, then you can deliver the reality to match. A big part of achieving that reality resides in how you deliver service.

The legendary Leonard L. Berry is a University Distinguished Professor of Marketing and a Regents Professor in the Mays Business School at Texas A&M University. He has been a friend and inspiration for 40 years and is considered one of the most accomplished marketing educators in the world. He is a former president of the American Marketing Association and has written 10 books on the power of service excellence throughout the years.

Len is one of the foremost academic experts in service marketing, which also happened to be one of the disciplines in which our firm excelled. Different from product marketing, selling and servicing the intangible was the primary focus of his extensive research and collaboration across the decades. He was one of the masterminds behind the original service quality research, created multiple quality service models, and gave many a speech on the *Lessons of Great Service*.

Len understands how the landscape of customer service and the entire CX model is undergoing a massive paradigm shift. He knows full well that companies currently boasting about customer centricity still have a hard time turning those values and plans into action. In a recent vodcast with host Liam Geraghty,[3] Len points out that

---

3 Liam Geraghty, "Leonard Berry and the Eternal Pursuit of Service Excellence," *Intercom* (September 21, 2023), https://www.intercom.com/blog/videos/leonard-berry-customer-service-excellence.

successful companies respect their customers, make them central to their operations, allocate resources based on their needs, and strive to exceed their expectations. He goes on to say that, in order to attain service excellence in an increasingly AI-driven world, it's key to balance high-tech solutions with high-touch interactions, where AI complements rather than replaces people. His bottom line: If you want your reality to be raving fan customers, then consistently great service is at the core.

ONE MIND SPACE

Guiding clients to better align their markets' perception and reality over the years has taught me one thing for certain: Your customers have only one mind space for your brand. Just one. I call it the *point of alignment*. It is that singular point where everything relevant to your brand image comes together and connects.

The point of alignment is that singular point where everything relevant to your brand image comes together and connects.

Think about the one mind space you have in your brain for a brand—any brand. If I say, "Starbucks," you have one immediate thought. It might be *warm and cozy atmosphere* or *overroasted and burnt*, or *my favorite coffee*, or even *I wouldn't go in there if you bought my coffee for me*. Those instant, singular responses and perceptions

29

are generated from a collection of impressions. They are usually garnered at the beginning of the brand relationship and, over time, through experiences that either nurtured or demolished your perception of the brand.

All in, you still have only one mind space for them. You don't afford them multiple mind spaces for different categories. It wouldn't make sense to hold two instantly contradictory images in your mind for the same brand. For example, you eat at an Italian restaurant named Luigi's that also happens to serve BBQ. What are you going to know them for? Pick one. It doesn't mean you can't have multiple thoughts about a brand once you start thinking about it, but you only have one instant mind space. You are too busy, and your mind is too full of other brands to store multiple mind spaces for any one brand. In fact, recent estimates claim that, whether you know it or not, you process over 10,000 brands a day, one way or the other. Unless you work at or have ownership in a brand, you only spend one mind space on them. That would make the challenge for Starbucks, Luigi's, or any brand, to fill that one mind space with the right perception simultaneously supported by an aligned delivery. Any gap between the two will shift the alignment.

Your customers have only one mind space for your brand.

A keen understanding of your buyer's mindset is critical to proper brand alignment.

Knowing your customers' expectations allows you to better understand the one mind space they have for your brand. Once you have that understanding, make sure you fill their one mind space with the one thing that will bring their perception in line with the reality you deliver. What is that one thing your team, your partners, and your customers can rally around that makes immediate common sense? Where is your point of alignment? How will you fill that one mind space?

A decade after I had started my first firm, the hit movie *City Slickers* was released. It included a scene that made it much easier for me to help others understand a key point to successful branding. *City Slickers* is an American comedy Western film starring Billy Crystal, Daniel Stern, Bruno Kirby, and—last but most important to the branding world—Jack Palance. Jack played Curly, a rough and rugged old cowboy who was always snickering at Mitch's (played by Billy Crystal) citified perspective on life. Consistently confused about where his life in New York City was headed, Mitch finally mustered up the courage to ask Curly about the secret of life. Leaning over his horse and holding one crooked old index finger in the air, Curly offered his sage wisdom: "One thing. It all comes down to one thing. You focus on that, and everything else don't mean shit." Still confused, Mitch asks him what that one thing is. Curly quips back: "That's what you gotta figure out." The scene ends with Billy Crystal staring at his own index finger and wondering about the *one thing*. I have encountered more than a few entrepreneurs who are still staring at their index finger.

What makes your enterprise great? What makes your business magical? Without nailing down that one thing, none of your execution strategies will ever achieve their true potential. Knowing your customers are only going to give you one mind space, what are you going to fill it with? What is your point of alignment?

THE POWER OF AN ALIGNED BRAND

When a brand is able to create an emotional connection with its stakeholders that goes well beyond the practical functionality of its product or service, it creates multiple advantages for the company. It generates increased sales, inspires loyalty, and cultivates hard-earned trust. When the buying experience is a pure joy for the customer, you will usually find impeccable alignment between the brand promise and its delivery. When it flows well, it provides the customer an enjoyable, seamless process where everything just makes sense. It actually gets to the point where your customer wants to spend more money with you just because it feels good. In a world where so many other brands are letting them down, you become the bright spot in their day because you deliver. In doing so, you also lower price sensitivity, sharpen your competitive edge, and make it far easier to generate exponential referrals.

Other areas of benefit for an aligned brand include an easier introduction platform from which to launch new products or services, enhanced customer retention, and a higher return on all of your advertising and social media spends. Last but not least, it is contagious to your culture, which ultimately cycles back to improving your overall business alignment. In a time where more than half of workforce employees say they're disengaged at work and relatively dissatisfied with their jobs,[4] creating a positive culture so your team members can engage with your brand on a meaningful level is paramount to a better overall environment. There is no reason not to treat your team, regardless of size, with the same intentionality you do your customers. The customers have a customer experience journey, so why shouldn't your workers have their journey? Align your brand with the team experience journey and watch productivity explode.

TIME TO PEE: BUC-EE'S ALIGNED BRAND

How long can you hold it? This is an incredible story of an entrepreneur who found the hidden opportunity to turn clean bathrooms into an enormous brand cult. While I did not create the Buc-ee's brand, the owner is a friend who has a story that exemplifies Brand ON! To be clear, Buc-ee's concept was never really what I consider Brand OFF! Like all of us entrepreneurs, they certainly had their survival and growth battles from day one, but their vision for the future was spot on from the start. How they got there is what makes it a cool story.

In 1982, Arch "Beaver" Aplin III found an empty piece of property by a four-way stop sign between his blue-collar hometown of Lake Jackson, Texas, and neighboring Clute. He purchased the property from a Houston businessman and then proceeded to use

---

4 Megan Cerullo, "More than Half of Employees Are Disengaged, or 'Quiet Quitting' Their Jobs," *Moneywatch* (June 13, 2023), https://www.cbsnews.com/news/workers-disengaged-quiet-quitting-their-jobs-gallup.

his construction science degree to help him build a convenience store. His vision was to upsize the industry average store from 2,400 square feet to 3,000 square feet and finish out the shop in a little bit nicer accompaniments than the average pump and munch. He was telling everyone he knew how much nicer his convenience store would be and encouraging them to please stop by.

Early in the process, Arch had decided he wanted a special name and logo he could use to build on in the future. He drew his inspiration from the fact his childhood nickname was Bucky Beaver, his dog was named Buck, and his Brazoswood High School mascot was the Buccaneers. He knew he wanted to name the new store Buc-ee's and was adamant about creating a cartoon character logo of a beaver to go with it. While the artwork was not ready by his store opening, he had already hired someone to bring his dream to life, so he slapped some Buc-ee's basic lettering on a white banner and pinned it to the eave of the building.

The original concept was a success, but how would he expand on it? Prior to opening up his second store, Aplin brought on a partner, Don Wasek, who was another local convenience store owner with extensive financing and retail experience. Don's father was in the beverage distribution business and was well versed in the retail and supply chain sectors, giving Don a perfect background to partner with Beaver. Over 20 years later, the two men's complementary skill sets and ambition had driven them to open 20 stores, mostly in the Brazoria County area of Texas.

But by 2003, Beaver and his partner had come to understand the primary reason people stopped at roadside gas stations was to go to the restroom. These restrooms were usually borderline nasty and often unavailable. Much of the time, fuel was actually a secondary reason for the stop and snacks a third. He thought, *What would happen if we offered really large, sparkling clean restrooms for all travelers?* It was his belief the number of visitors would be tied directly to having clean, comfortable, safe places for all to go to the restroom. With that concept in mind, they opened their first travel center concept on Interstate 10 in Luling, Texas. They more than doubled the 3,000 footprint to an 8,500 foot size, only to double it again three years later to a behemoth 17,000 square feet, which, by the way, doubled again soon after. While most gas stations had one very dirty men's and one slightly dirty women's restroom at that time, Buc-ee's locations sported anywhere from a massive 20–50 glistening clean commodes and urinals. A venerable bathroom heaven for travelers. Beaver thought he might have found that *one thing.*

To launch the highway versions of Buc-ee's bathroom-driven concepts, Aplin and Wasek decided on a highway billboard advertising strategy. They generated awareness of the brand with the unique approach of highlighting their clean restrooms with such creative quips like, "You can hold it!" Another original favorite was, "Your throne awaits." The Houston ad firm of Stan & Lou did a remarkable job of launching the brand on billboards, and interest in the unique travel center concept began to grow from highway to highway, town to town.

Just in case you are one of the rare few who has not stopped by a Buc-ee's, allow me to give you a taste of their brand alignment success. Better yet, after you read my description, go to their website at buc-ees.com to see the aura I am trying to describe. It is all so very well done.

One usually starts the Buc-ee's customer journey process with the aforementioned billboards, which they have continued to creatively use to entertain and entice drivers for years. Then there is the giant red, white, and yellow circular beaver logo sign we all look for on a singular pole way up in the sky. It lets you know exits in advance when you need to plan to get off the highway to experience Buc-ee's bliss. Upon entering the parking lot, you will have at least 100 gas pumps to choose from if you need fuel for your vehicle, with some locations touting as many as 120 pumps. When you pull up to one, it is clean as can be and will have meaningful instructional signage, all branded, as well as employee benefit recruitment signage. The reason they put the branded employee pay info right in front of you is not just to recruit more team members but to help you understand why all of their employees are so damn friendly. I don't care whether it is the guy sweeping the parking lot, the person constantly cleaning the potties, or the wonderful smiling woman at the bakery serving you a hot kolache, they are all happy. They all make you feel welcomed and appreciated.

Upon filling up your car, you go inside the Mecca. It is huge. It is bright. It is so clean it sparkles. As soon as you enter the door and walk past one of the many giant checkout lanes, someone will greet you with a "Welcome to Buc-ee's!" and they mean it. The next visual you will get is a landscape of color, merchandise, food, and bustling activity as far as you can see. Once you step into the flow, you've got to keep moving. If you need to use the restroom, know that is in and of itself a branded treat. Everything has a logo on it. Then back in the store, everything is a beaver, but it's not overdone. It has a certain touch to it. If you are lucky, you may get to meet the live full-size mascot beaver walking around the store for photo ops, which as you know by now, end up all over the internet.

All of their food is fantastic. From the fresh sliced BBQ to the homemade fudge, it's all good. While they carry your favorite national brands on their massive shelves, they also have integrated their private Buc-ee's branded items throughout the store. I usually stay away from white label products at any store because they are typically lower quality than the branded ones, but not at Buc-ee's. Their private labeled stuff is as good and, in some cases, better than the national brands. Trust that the beaver logo is all over those items and, in fact, anywhere you turn in that store. Just head over to the toy section, which you will do if you have kids or grandkids with you, and choose from many different sizes of the branded stuffed beaver character, beaver coloring books, or lunch boxes. In the end, you will find yourself leaving with a basket load of goodies and will be properly thanked on your way out the door. Full stomach, full gas tank, empty bladder, and empty wallet: Buc-ee's has perfect brand alignment from start to finish.

Buc-ee's has perfect brand alignment from start to finish.

Buc-ee's brand alignment story doesn't end here. The highly successful chain has grown to a current total of 50 travel centers with 36 locations in Texas plus 14 stores dotting the Southeast in Alabama, Florida, South Carolina, Kentucky, and Tennessee. Their sales exceed a gazillion dollars a year. Aplin and his team deserve all the accolades for being one of the rare examples I can provide of perfect brand alignment. Beaver found that one thing and rode it to success. Buc-ee's is officially Brand ON! Acclaimed.

⚡

Beaver found that one thing and rode it to success.

What is your one thing? Do you know your point of alignment? What are you known for or want to be known for? Are you effectively filling that one mind space with it? Is every single touchpoint of your brand in alignment with that one thing?

CHAPTER 3

Brand OFF!

If you are not Brand ON!, you are Brand OFF! Look around you. How many brands did you encounter in the last week you could tell are out of alignment? A missed service opportunity here or a poorly delivered product there—was it a misplaced communication or an average experience with a business you secretly hoped would be better than average? What was the last brand to disappoint you? How did they scar that one mind space you had for them?

One that promptly comes to mind is my fried chicken story. If you're from the South, you know it's hard to beat a great Southern fried chicken dinner. What images does a Southern fried chicken dinner bring to your mind? The smell of sizzling, crunchy fried chicken, the taste of creamy mashed potatoes, and fluffy buttered biscuits? Yum. You can smell it now, right? Now imagine you walk into the best fried chicken restaurant you know, and you smell FISH!

My personal favorite fast-food fried chicken joint for years was Chicken Fast (the name was changed a bit to protect their brand), now a franchise chain. Their brand was totally in alignment. Everything about their customer experience was perfect. They served scrumptious fried chicken and all the appropriate sides with a flair for good service. No matter which location I visited, I was always guaranteed an incredibly clean restaurant, friendly service, and the aromatic smell and tasty flavor of their extraordinary fried chicken. I can't even begin to tell you how many boxes of their chicken I purchased through the years since the opening of their first store.

But then came the unthinkable. Someone at the top of their outfit decided to start offering fried fish at many of their locations. I'm sorry, isn't your name *Chicken* Fast? The very first time I went into my favorite fried chicken place and smelled fish, I was done. Perhaps you think that is extreme, but that is how brand alignment works. Did the increase in their business from the sale of fish outpace the number of chicken customers they lost due to the smell of the fish? I hope so, but seriously doubt it. They will probably never know. Fast-food franchises usually don't reach out to say, "Gee, we haven't seen you in forever. Is everything OK? Why aren't you eating here anymore?" Nope, customers just quit going, and they lose the business. They opened up the one mind space I had for them, which originally said, "Great fried chicken fast," and changed it to "Stinky fried fish near my chicken! Don't go again." I am sure this particular chain fries their fish in a different vat of hot grease than their chicken, but so what? Perception is reality. I love fried fish too, but I don't want it anywhere near my chicken. Now another chicken place has taken over my fried chicken mind space and my cash, and they don't sell fish.

HOW YOU KNOW YOUR BRAND IS OUT OF ALIGNMENT

It's not always as easy as the fried fish example. While on many occasions, it is a very obvious blunder, it can also be something you must discern over time, such as different members of your team describing your products or services differently, customers appearing confused when making buying decisions or placing orders, or you having trouble sharing your company values or story in a consistent manner. Online, it could be a high bounce or abandon rate on your website or shopping cart telling you something is not kosher. On your social posts or ads, it could be a low CTR (click-through rate), or there may be a big discrepancy between your brick-and-mortar and online appearance.

More obvious signs are that you may be attracting customers who are not actually the type of customers you want, indicating you have a disconnect with your audience. Team members not advocating your brand like they believe in it or a high product return rate are solid indicators as well. Graphically, you may appear inconsistent across different platforms, and content-wise, you may not be speaking in a tone that is congruent with your desired image. Or maybe it's as clear as a significant drop in sales or traffic. There are so many indications your brand is struggling to be in alignment, and once you know what to look for, you will begin seeing more of them if there is an issue.

HOW POTHOLES KNOCK BRANDS OUT OF ALIGNMENT

Think about how your car drives. When it's in perfect alignment, it rolls effortlessly down the road, providing you smooth handling and peak performance. When your wheels are not in alignment, the car gives you a significantly rougher ride while putting unnecessary stress on the car and uneven wear on the tires. Every day you choose to wait to get your wheels aligned, you will endure one more day of an uncomfortable ride. Likewise, for every day you delay getting your brand in alignment, you experience another day of lost opportunity. You may ultimately get to where you are going, but the ride won't be nearly as smooth, as fast, or as profitable as it would with everything in alignment.

Potholes take your car out of alignment. Hit just one pothole at speed and your car begins to wobble. Drive bumpy roads consistently, and your car will struggle to perform at its best. Likewise, your business hits potholes for various reasons, and they will take your brand out of alignment. Over the years, I kept a running list of these underlying reasons, and seven of them come up time and time again. These are the Top 7 Potholes that destroy brand alignment. My assumption is that you will find one or more that hits close to home, but most of the time, they sneak up on leaders. Keep in mind that this is not a comprehensive list of every underlying reason a brand gets knocked out of alignment, but they are the most prominent. Also, this list does not include the profusion of tactical errors companies make due to these underlying causes. Have any of these turned your Brand OFF?

The Top 7 Potholes

- Internal marketing employees
- External marketing vendors
- The owner's forest
- Personal pride and success
- Wrong brand or concept
- Compromising to please others
- Unintentional morphing

Internal Marketing Employees

This pothole could be an entire book one day. At first, it may seem hard to believe your brand's biggest enemy may well be your own internal marketing person or team of people, but it is true. Remember, marketing is not the sole driver of brand alignment, so sometimes the two are not in sync. Ask Bud Light. An internal marketing team member wanted to "push change" and gave birth to a political hot potato promotion using the services of a trans influencer during March Madness. Moreover, someone up top approved it. It cost AB InBev a fortune, and Bud Light lost its lead position in the marketplace.

There are far too many stories of misaligned marketing campaigns created within enterprises of all sizes. This unfortunate phenomenon is quite common for a myriad of reasons. In fact, if you have a marketing person or team in place and your brand is in alignment, you are the exception and should be grateful. Take them out to dinner tonight and thank them. That is what I do in the rare instance I am working with a client and find their internal marketing team to be spot on with brand alignment. I don't have to buy many dinners.

The main reason internal marketing employees are often a big pothole is quite simple: Their job and their paycheck depend on your happiness. That may sound obvious, but they work to please you, and they can read the room. They know full well the things you like and don't like. They grasp your propensity to select one strategy or tactic over another, and at the end of the day, you are the boss. Many critical marketing and branding decisions are compromised in this manner, resulting in an overall program that is, quite frankly, very mediocre. Sure, there might be moments of brilliance, but evaluated over the long term, you are most certainly not maximizing your potential.

Their pride of authorship is the second most prevalent reason internal marketing can create a problem. This challenge runs rampant in our industry because internal employees ultimately want the program to be their idea. They want their name on it. They want to be your hero. Again, it ties back into pleasing you, and they will run through walls to put their stamp on something they feel can gain them favor. It's human nature, but it does not help your brand alignment. These marketing workers aren't intentionally dragging down your program or taking your brand out of alignment, but do you really think they are going to challenge you very hard? Will they stand up to you and tell you no? Will they tell you your baby is ugly and you need to change its name? You need to seriously consider the fact that their heart is never where yours is unless you have based their compensation on an equity share of your business. Even then, they may not understand brand alignment and your best opportunities for success.

Third is just a lack of relevant experience. Where has your internal marketing leader gained their experience? Are they able to draw from years of practice in other industries, or have they only worked in your discipline? How many years have they been out of school, and where did they go to school? The critical baseline knowledge necessary to be a competent marketing talent is taught in the best business schools, but the most important skill sets needed to be a great brand leader are learned on the streets.

Finally, most internal marketing people are not strategic business thinkers and are much more comfortable in the deployment of marketing tactics. For smaller businesses, this could mean a quick pop in sales but a long-term misalignment of the brand. Simply put, strategic thinking looks at the vision and overall goals of the company, while tactics are the various activities implemented to support the strategies. Tactics are what keep most internal marketing people busy—along with their side hustle!

Many of today's business owners feel like any kid with a smartphone is capable of marketing. Sometimes they are, and they can light up your social accounts, but that tactic doesn't necessarily bode well for the long-term viability of your brand. Social media will probably play a big role in developing your brand, but who is making that decision and providing strategic guidance? Just because someone has *marketing* next to their name does not mean they know anything about branding, much less the alignment of your brand.

Just because someone has marketing next to their name does not mean they know anything about branding.

Last on this topic, if you have a really talented marketing leader working for you, chances are they will be bored stiff in less than two years. Historically, the average tenure for an internal marketing employee is very short. They have seen and done everything for your small business by their 18th month, and it is difficult for you to continue to challenge them. Truly great marketing people want to be continually challenged to climb the next mountain, create the next great brand, or launch the next award-winning advertising or social campaign. That is why the predominance of the most talented marketing employees are working for ad agencies or running their own firms. The select few internal marketing employees who have legitimate talent and are disciplined enough to follow a well-defined brand alignment strategy are hard to find and worth their weight in gold.

External Marketing Vendors

In similar fashion to their internal counterparts, external marketing vendors can create major potholes as well. They also want to please. They too want to put their name on the concept. More than anything, however, they want to sell. They want to sell you more media space, more production time, more web development, more printing, more design work, more search engine optimization work, and so on. Again, it's human nature, but it is your brand.

Take a case that happened to me on a recent rebrand I lead for a successful $20 million business. It was a major rebrand, including renaming the company, developing an entirely new look and feel, producing and launching a new television campaign, new radio spots, new social, new website, revisiting all internal processes, thoroughly examining the entire customer journey, and launching it all in a scant four months. The brand was now aligned, and the early results were going through the roof. Everyone could not have been happier because everything looked great, and expectations were being exceeded.

More than anything, external marketing vendors want to sell.

Upon completion of the work and our exit from the project, I left the client with certain pearls of wisdom. One such pearl was to warn them of these Top 7 Potholes. Lo and behold, just 30 days after our launch, with calls and results pouring in, a radio media salesman went to the internal marketing director and recommended new radio spots. Even though the new spots we completed had only been launched 30 days earlier and were highly successful, he was of the opinion the client needed to change their commercials every few weeks. He convinced the internal marketing person, who convinced the business owner, and off they went. Ultimately, the spots were a disaster and never ran. When they called me with the story, I simply asked if they had inquired how many brands this radio rep had created and launched in his life. The call went silent when they realized this was one of the pieces of wisdom I had shared during my exit.

The Owner's Forest

Among the trees is where it is hardest to see the forest. Of the hundreds of clients I have counseled in my career, almost all of them were individually far smarter than me. They had created great companies and organizations built on products or services that were changing industries and lives. They were—and still are—brilliant leaders and courageous entrepreneurs who put their money down and their lives on the line. They sacrificed, sweated, and relentlessly invested themselves and their families into their dream and made it work. In doing so, however, many times, they were far too deep among those trees to see the forest.

Working with so many owners throughout the years, it became crystal clear the main reason they had created their own pothole is because they were too close to their baby. When you invest so much into something and spend a ton of time thinking and talking about it, it becomes nearly impossible to be objective, much less creative, and see the brand how others see it. Quite often, my magic solution for their brand alignment situation was a very slight and obvious change of course, one they just could not see on their own. Or if they did see it, they were too stubborn to address it. It reminds me of one very successful gentleman who said boisterously at the start of his project, "You can recommend anything, but we will not change our name." After changing their name and blowing their results out of the water, he acquiesced. Sometimes you just need to have someone help you step back from the trees to see the forest.

Sometimes you just need to have someone help you step back from the trees to see the forest.

Entrepreneurial tunnel vision, similar to the never-ending trees, is about the tunnel we entrepreneurs crawl into when we give birth to an idea. We become hyper focused on what we are creating and how we dream it will play out in the future. It becomes hard for us to listen to the harsh reality outsiders may be trying to share with us. While we inherently know outside influences could have a profound impact on our business, we still may not want to hear them. In short, it becomes difficult to see the big picture.

This occurs frequently when the topic of branding surfaces. Whether it's naming a company or a product, you have a vision for what you think it should be called or how it will be positioned in the market. Perhaps you are right, and you are one of the few geniuses who absolutely understood your market and how they would experience your brand. You were able to get out of your own tunnel, see everything the way the market sees it, and move beyond your true area of expertise, and you nailed it! Congrats. That does occur from time to time, but more often not.

A couple of tunnel vision professional examples I like to share are engineers and doctors, two of the smartest groups of people I have been honored to work with in my business life. The engineer will create a new technical marvel product, which my team and I could barely comprehend, and, oh, by the way, he also knows how to brand it because everyone understands how he thinks. No, very few of us can understand how you think, so you better make darn sure you have someone translate your brilliance into a brand people want to believe in. But it is their baby, so the predominance of our engagement is spent trying to get the engineer outside of his own tunnel.

There is a long-running witticism in the marketing world that doctors live on their own pedestals and will occasionally come down to talk to you. Granted, they save lives. They make people better. They keep us healthy. They went to school for a really long time. They are usually much smarter than we are, and their sense of piousness is often well deserved. But when it comes to branding, stand back, because they are experts at that as well, making it incredibly hard to get them out of their entrepreneurial tunnel. It's really hard telling a surgeon who just made $50,000 for a single surgery what he needs to do to improve the brand he is trying to grow. Docs will usually begin ramping up their private practice with early success purely because of their immense talent, but they face difficulty trying to extrapolate that into a larger business model. The maturity growth cycle catches up with them, and their unique medical forte is not enough to drive the numbers they desire, so they eventually come out of their tunnel to listen, or their practice stagnates.

Personal Pride and Success

This one gets us all. It's a rush to lay claim to a brand, marketing, or advertising idea, because it is out in the public eye for everyone to see. It's as close as most of us ever get to Hollywood, and our pride swells up when we see our idea on TV or a billboard. It is simply cool to see your thoughts traveling down the freeway on the side of a big truck or on a product on the grocery store shelves. Even if it is just a graphic on a banner at the company picnic, it feels all warm inside for the person who believes they created it. It is one of the reasons social media has taken off like it has. Everyone gets to be a creator, writer, designer, publisher, broadcaster, or influencer. People get a huge rush out of seeing their own work on the screen, regardless of how good it is—or is not.

The funny thing is, most ideas are not original. I will not bore you by listing the scores of ad campaign slogans recycled throughout time by different advertisers, but I will give you one example. How many times have you seen the campaign, *We ARE [name goes here]. We ARE Penn State. We ARE Virginia Tech. We ARE St. Louis. We ARE Washington. We ARE Missouri.* And so on. It's pride running rampant. Exactly how does that differentiate you? Someone actually got paid to "create" that stuff, and—even worse—someone else approved it.

Personal pride naturally compels many business owners to create their own brands. Perhaps their daughter, son, or wife had the idea. It becomes a cocktail topic at the bar and gives business leaders bragging rights. Sometimes those approaches turn out just fine, but most of the time, they don't. I remember listening to the CEO of an oil field company for 30 minutes tell me how the brand he had created for his company was enormously successful. He told me how much time it took for his daughter to design the company logo and how proud of it all he was. They sold BOPs (that's a blowout preventer for those of you not familiar with the oil field) ranging from tens of thousands to hundreds of thousands of dollars each. Once he was through pontificating, he asked me the leading question, "So what do you think of my baby?" I can tell you from experience that is like stepping into the loaded question from your wife, "How do you like my new hairstyle honey?" Damned if you do, and damned if you don't. I said, "Sir, your baby is ugly, and you need to change its name." Believe it or not, I successfully counseled that client for a very long time.

Success is often a major personal pride pothole on the road to brand alignment. Most of our brand alignment projects are not about helping failing companies; rather, they're about maximizing the potential of already successful ones. Therefore, the initiatives usually include overcoming the virtues and challenges of that existing success. Breaking brand paradigms is usually easier in a struggling company than it is in a successful one, because the leaders, on average, are ready to listen. Small business leaders already experiencing financial success might tend to be a bit more guarded in their approach to new ideas relating to brand alignment.

Let's not just talk about revenues and profits but the actual joy of running the business and serving others. How do you define success? What was your expectation of your brand when you started your work? Are your customers, clients, or patients raving fans? Do they thoroughly enjoy doing business with your organization? Is it a seamless experience that keeps them coming back for more, more frequently? Is it an experience they feel compelled to share with others because of the pure pleasure of doing business with you? Is leading your business a joy for you?

Success only becomes a pothole if you let it. It becomes an obstacle when you use it as an excuse to not think out of the proverbial box or challenge yourself to be better. It also becomes a hurdle when you use it as a reason not to change or adjust with shifts in the marketplace. Now more than ever, markets are rapidly changing, and businesses are moving at the speed of light. Don't let success slow you down.

Wrong Brand or Concept

There are so many things to consider when starting or growing a business. Many times, leaders feel like brand is something secondary to engineering, production, finance, or human resources. Sometimes, entrepreneurs do not have the time or the contacts they really need to launch their brand, so they either table it for later or reach out to their easiest access point. They go to a friend who knew someone who had a kid that graduated in marketing, or they search online for a branding firm in their area or on trusted online sources for long-distance counsel. Any of that can work if you are lucky enough to connect with one of the few real experts in the industry, but you usually don't get that lucky.

I once asked a new client how he determined the name of his company. He said they really couldn't come up with one themselves so they hired a marketing company. He noted that the first several concepts the marketing company presented were not any good and the process became so frustrating they decided to just go with one they had originally presented so they could get started. Ouch. They proceeded to use the improper and irrelevant name for six years before they decided it was time to address the elephant in the room. Regardless, they were financially successful by all metrics, but when we took care of the elephant, their business exploded.

If you acquire a company or take a position in a company you did not create, you may not have had a choice in the brand, so you are saddled with the challenge of leveraging a brand that may not have been right from the start. Don't let that sway you. You may have to address the board of directors, a partner, or investors, but address them you should, so you can do what you need to do to get the brand in alignment.

A bad business concept doesn't require a lot of discussion. If the business concept does not make sense, brand alignment will not save it. Sure, we have been asked to put lipstick on some proverbial pigs, but we always chose not to if the business model did not make sense. You can make an idea or an organization look really good for a given period of time, but at some point, performance must meet or exceed expectations. If your business concept or model does not work, call it a day, and move on to the next idea that gives you a chance for success.

— ⚡ —

If the business concept does not make sense, brand alignment will not save it.

Compromising to Please Others

Compromising to please others is a common road hazard capable of destroying your tires and making your car wobble. Family members, partners, advisors, friends, board members, employees, and other influencers will all weigh in on your brand. Remember, everyone is an expert when it comes to marketing. Ever since the personal computer hit the shelves in the 1980s, I have witnessed a growing number of experts in marketing and branding. Anyone can design a logo now, and AI can write copy for you. Actually, you don't have to think at all to be a marketing director or advisor. There is so much to cover on this topic from so many angles. I will summarize by sharing one piece of wisdom I am absolutely certain about after 50 years in the marketing and branding world; great branding is *never* done by committee.

Even though there is good reason to seek input from others, make sure you keep it at just that: input. Do not let the brand alignment decision-making process fall into the category of a group project. If you do, know in advance that you will end up with mediocre results at best. Trying to please everyone when branding or rebranding is totally impossible. You have to lead.

Great branding is *never* done by committee.

I will never forget making a major marketing and advertising presentation in front of 150 top doctors who were all part of a very successful and well-established medical center. We were laying out the strategies for their brand along with the advertising campaign we recommended implementing. When listing the television and radio stations we recommended as part of our media buy, one of the preeminent surgeons in the world stood up and loudly said, "Mr. Coleman, with all due respect, I do not listen to a single radio station you are recommending." A quick scan of the large room brought forth an image of me being Custer at Little Big Horn as all the docs had folded their arms awaiting my response. I returned fire stating, "Doctor, with all due respect, sir, I am not after your business," referring to the fact I did not need to reach him by radio.

You may well have to answer to a board of directors or group of savvy investors. Know they all come to the table with different prejudices from other businesses that will sway the way they think about or react to your brand alignment direction. Just make sure your brand alignment is intimately crafted to your marketplace, and clearly articulate how your stakeholders will benefit from your commitment to that market.

For those of you in a family business, you know there are no tougher arenas to instigate or launch than a brand alignment initiative. Dan Baker was one of the top family business counselors in the country for many years. He authored numerous books, including *What Happy People Know* and *What Happy Companies Know*. He consulted with notable family businesses across many industries and would bring me in at the first mention of the word *brand*. He understood the challenges we faced to make progress in an established family business, especially when there was a generation or two of success and the young people in the room knew the brand needed to change to match the modern marketplace. Man did the sparks fly!

Dr. Baker taught me how to navigate compromise among family members without losing sight of the clients' ultimate business goals. He also shared the intrinsic value of honest, direct communication in tough situations. I must tell you we had a lot of fun and success in such ventures, even though most of our time was spent refereeing and redirecting as opposed to managing and brand counseling. The rewards for those families, and for Dan and me, were immense. It was truly some of the most enjoyable work of my lifetime.

It brings to mind a consulting engagement in New York City with one of the nation's premier seafood houses, which is owned by a prominent family. This great company provides the freshest seafood, gourmet cheeses, dry-aged steaks, and many other market delicacies throughout New York City, the Hamptons, and now, thanks to their website, the entire country. Amazing food, great knowledge and delivery, all owned by a father whose son wanted nothing to do with the spectacularly successful business. Yet dad wanted to build a family legacy brand. Tough alignment. Tough assignment. In the end, the brand alignment initiative was very helpful in aligning the family, because it got everyone rowing in the same direction.

To wrap up compromise, I want to focus on your employees again. More often than not, we underappreciate the radical changes in company culture where today's leaders need to bring a sensibility about people's demands and emotional maturity that is driving many organizations. With a workplace where needs are radically changing, it is up to leadership to encourage their team to support their organizations' brand alignment. Obviously, buy-in is desired across the board, but in reality, you do not need 100% approval of all employees. There are many different reasons some employees will never buy into your brand alignment, and many times, those select individuals will just need to find another job. Some don't want change and love to say, "We have never done it that way before." Boy is that gasoline on my fire! Some will adamantly state, "I don't want to do it that way," which is a whole other issue in today's climate. Select individuals believe their job responsibilities will change and more will be required of them. They are comfortable and don't want you moving their cheese. It is vitally important to remember that, at the end of the day, you are the person responsible for the brand's success. You don't necessarily have to create the brand, but you definitely have to lead the charge. What I have learned from the truly great leaders in this scenario is, if you will actually lead, they will follow. Remember, great branding is never done by committee.

Unintentional Morphing

It is uncanny how often this seventh pothole blows a tire. While the term *morphing* is used regularly to describe an organization's intentional transformation process, unintentional morphing is a natural but unwanted brand phenomenon that can sneak up on even the best leaders. This gradual, almost imperceptible change can be driven by a pressure for performance, desire to jump ahead of the competition, fear of missing out on opportunities, or simply keeping up with the latest market trends, which can spin a brand totally out of alignment.

A sure road sign that your brand is morphing out of alignment is when individual members of your team are describing your brand differently. Maybe you have had staff turnover or simply failed to establish a consistent training methodology. One team member describes your product or services to a customer one way, and another team member describes them in their own way. This creates immediate confusion with your customers. This confusion is a major indicator your brand is dangerously out of alignment. Your prospective and current customers go to your website, social, and other marketing materials to get a sense of who you are and what you are all about. If they don't line up with what your people are telling them, the customer will quickly choose another brand. Your messaging must be clear and consistent across all platforms and must align with the promise of your organization. Remember, one mind space.

Inconsistent delivery is another sign of morphing. In an attempt to continually improve, leaders will often change things. Some changes make sense, some do not. Some attempted improvements are mere busy work. One thing is for sure, the more uncertainty you create for your customers the more out of alignment your brand is. Inconsistent delivery creates doubt and yields lost opportunity.

BRAND ALIGNMENT FAILURE

A prime example of brand alignment failure is a restaurant group who came to us with lagging sales and loss of direction. They were a well-known, all-day casual dining concept with a solid reputation for great breakfasts, but the rest of the day's food was pretty medio-cre. Very successful with their first locations in their headquarter city, they began growing and branching out into other cities. As they expanded, the owners began shifting more of the decisions to operations people and store managers. Meanwhile, they were paying less and less attention to the subtleties that were occurring to their brand while they were focused on the financials.

It was back in the day when salad bars were a relatively new concept being installed in some restaurants, so the corporate director of operations thought they needed to have one of those to resolve their lackluster lunch and dinner numbers. It was the classic "solution in search of a problem" scenario. They also originally had a counter bar with dining stools where people loved sitting when they were eating alone. Well, someone had the bright idea that the beloved counter took the "sophistication" out of the place, which kept the diners away at lunch and dinner. One of the managers decided to initiate a menu change, while the guy across town thought focusing on a line of ice cream would improve their karma. Two of the owners thought it needed a name change, but the third blamed slow adoption in other cities on the interior design of the eatery. You get my point. What they ended up with was nothing like where they started. They outthought themselves away from what worked and became something that didn't. The brand was morphing into misalignment and they couldn't see it.

It didn't end there. We presented them with a total brand realignment concept to get them back to what made them great: breakfast. At the time, there were not many all-day breakfast chains operating in Texas (Cracker Barrel wasn't there yet), and it was a blossoming market. The realignment included a total makeover, a name change, and more importantly, taking advantage of the fact there are a lot of people who love to eat breakfast items throughout the day.

They thought the entire concept was perfect. "It's approved. Let's do it!" claimed one owner. So they agreed to ditch the salad bars, put the counters back in, eliminate most of the nonbreakfast items from the menu, elevate the quality of the breakfast fare, and launch a major ad campaign to announce the rebrand.

This rather large initiative would also require some healthy remodeling at several of the locations, which was to be implemented while we were producing all of the new branding materials and advertising campaign. When it came to project management, we asked for the task of overseeing the remodel of the six restaurants in our home city so we could map progress. The ops guy insisted he had that under control and did not need our help with that part of the project, so we reluctantly took it out of our scope of work.

Fast forward six months to 30 days before the launch of the campaign. The "Country Breakfast" approach was going to be a home run. We had a Sam Elliott –kind of voice on the radio spots, with the sound of sizzling bacon in the background. It was so well done you could smell it through your car radio. Matching billboards were being erected, direct mail pieces around each restaurant were sent out, and newspaper ads were ready to run. We were higher than kites in anticipation, so we went to the location near our offices to eat breakfast and soak up the glory of a perfectly aligned brand. It looked fantastic! Everything was in perfect order. This was going to go down in history. It did.

I happened to be driving on the other side of town the next week and drove by one of the other locations. I walked in the front door with my chest all pumped up when all of a sudden a cold wave of shock smashed me in the face. They hadn't touched the physical aspects of this location. All they had done were the menu changes. The salad bar was still there. The counter was not. I felt that cold chill deep down in my bones and asked the manager, "What happened? Why isn't everything remodeled like we all agreed?"

The nice manager looked down as if he were the guilty one and said, "The owners decided to test your idea at only one location, the one by your offices, before they tried it on any of the others."

Needless to say, you can't run a major rebrand campaign across a big market to come to the "all new and improved country breakfast house" when only one of them was new and improved. I called the owners and asked why they took the shortcut. "Well, it was a major investment to remodel the others, and we didn't have the manpower at the time to manage it, so we decided to try it on one location," they murmured. I asked what they thought the customers who heard the radio spot and stopped in only to find nothing had really changed would think. Silence.

I suggested we stop the campaign, except in the neighborhood of the one location, and save the money and embarrassment I knew was about to happen. They ordered me to keep it all going, saying that the new menu alone would carry the success. Wrong. I hung up the phone, knowing our firm was in for our first large-scale failure in our 20-year existence.

The brand had unintentionally morphed, the owners had taken the steps to correct it, then cut the process short, and it totally fell on its butt. The chain ended up leaving that major city and retreating to their original concept, where they were comfortable. Many leaders don't recognize their business brand is morphing until it becomes costly to change it. It can occur from the owner's own fruition, requests by customers, or the well-meaning recommendation of various third parties.

Once a company's core focus falters and takes them away from what makes them great, the car starts to detour off the road. Some will morph slowly as this one did, while others will step on the accelerator and morph at the speed of light. Make note, unintentional morphing will destroy your business.

Unintentional morphing will destroy your business.

GET OUT OF YOUR OWN WAY!

As a business leader, you have to be able to get out of your own way. More often than not, that is the single biggest challenge my clients have faced. Truthfully, it's the single biggest challenge I have faced running my own firms. Whether it is seeing the forest for the trees, entrepreneurial tunnel vision, pride, or success, you have to be able to put those on a shelf to reach the next level. When you deal with successful people who have reached out to you because they want to be more successful, it creates a unique and often challenging paradigm. When the strongest recommendation you can give a client is to "get out of your own way," you are asking for pushback. You must then navigate that pushback to get them to their best selves in order to proceed in making a quantum difference in their business and personal lives.

As a business leader, you have to be able to get out of your own way.

It's always alarming when I hear, "Branding is just not my thing." Well, I get that, but you better find someone you trust whose thing it *is*. Proper brand alignment is so powerful you don't want to avoid it because you don't relate to or like marketing or branding. God made us all different and gave each of us unique skill sets so that we learn to depend on one another and, more importantly, on Him. I cannot tell you how many clients I've had to remind that they do not want me doing what they are great at doing. The engineer doesn't want me building bridges, and the surgeon most certainly does not want me operating on their patients. We all have expertise in something, so the key is learning where to align that expertise in the scope of your enterprise and finding the right someone to pay homage to your brand alignment. Stick to what you do best and hire the very best branding mind you can find to work with you.

How many of those major potholes have you hit? Did you hit them hard enough to take your car out of alignment? It only takes one. Are your wheels rolling smoothly down the road providing you a great ride, or is it time to take the car in to an expert?

CHAPTER 4

Brand ON!

Everyone loves success stories. Many business writers enjoy sharing stories about Nike, Coke, Apple, Microsoft, FedEx, or other giant companies, and I have great respect for their brand alignment challenges. However, I personally believe those examples are often overused in books trying to relate to entrepreneurs. I want to tell you the stories of smaller companies and organizations you may or may not have heard of, mom-and-pop entrepreneurs who did not know about the hidden power of brand alignment. Most of these businesses started out with humble beginnings, ran up against the wall, then made one key brand alignment decision that turned them into small business powerhouses who are not so small anymore.

---- ⚡ ----

These are small business powerhouses who are not so small anymore.

Each is in a totally unrelated business, yet they share the commonality of making a commitment to finding that single point of alignment and leveraging it to exceed customer expectations. In doing so, they powered up their revenues and became impact brands who have succeeded for decades. They became Brand ON!

Following each story is a brief highlight of the potholes responsible for taking their brand out of alignment and the overarching approach we took to identify and showcase their *one thing*, their point of alignment. The insight they garnered from the process set them on a path to success that helped them realize the dreams they had for their business. These were clients who were gracious enough to allow me to share their story, and every single one of them could be an entire book. All of them are uplifting beacons of hope and accomplishment.

HO HO HO! THE STORY OF SANTA'S WONDERLAND

There are three reasons I always start with Santa's Wonderland when it's time to tell a small business brand alignment success story where the owner "saw the light." First, it's really easy to see how brand alignment took their good concept and made it great. Second, their continual success over 25 years is nothing short of phenomenal, and third, they are owned by a wonderful family I personally respect and admire.

Brand OFF! Background

In 1998, entrepreneur Scott Medlin and his family decided to put some Christmas lights on the trees of a wooded area six miles south of College Station, Texas. Scott wholeheartedly believed in Christmas and wanted to share the joy of drive-through holiday lights with families located within their 20-mile radius. So he purchased the land, which was out in the middle of nowhere, and created a winding dirt road through the woods. He and his family then strung one million store-bought Christmas lights up in the trees and made various plywood ornamentations in their woodshop to create sparse holiday scenes throughout the would-be journey. The plan was for Land of Lights to charge $10 per carload to drive through the display, and that is how it all started.

The sparkling attraction drew the attention of passers-by, and cars started to come to see what the Christmas lights were all about. Patrons would pull up with station wagon–loads of kids filled with hope and excitement. The word started to spread, and the cars would line up on the shoulder of the highway, waiting for their turn to pull up to a two-man wooden hut, pay their $10, and drive their family slowly through the lights. The tour only encompassed a few acres and required a scant 15 minutes to drive through at speed. Nonetheless, Scott thoroughly enjoyed seeing the kids' happy faces pressed up against car windows taking in all of the sights.

At the end of the trail was a small area with a few old wooden buildings Medlin had inherited when he bought the property. He always thought they would be good for something, and by the fifth year, he decided to turn the old structures into a little Western town he named Tombstone. The area hosted a real campfire and staged a mock gunfight every hour or so. It was free for those who wanted to park their car and get out after viewing all of the lights. It was not a revenue generator and was actually more of an eyesore than an attraction, but it was there all the same. Gunfighting in a Western ghost town did not exactly align with the holiday spirit the Christmas lights were bringing. Regardless, cars were still lined up every year to drive through the lights, even though most did not take the time to stop at Tombstone. This business model was attracting roughly 10,000 cars a year and generating approximately $100,000 in annual revenue, not exactly Scott's dream but enough to keep the hope alive. Being an intuitive sort, he knew there was more opportunity for his concept but couldn't quite put his arms around what that looked like.

Brand ON! Realigning the Brand

In 2004, Scott called me in for a two-day Big Picture Thinking session, a whiteboard brainstorming retreat I would lead with him, his wife, and parents. I had some insight into his concept because, before I knew him, I had driven my kids through his Christmas light journey a year earlier and stopped by the uninviting Tombstone to see what it was all about. I distinctly remember telling my wife this was really weird and did not quite work with Christmas. I'm a cowboy at heart but still didn't think it was fitting for the kids to get all pumped up about Santa Claus only to finish the evening with four old gunslingers shooting each other to death in the dusty streets. The drive-through light tour was just good enough to keep our young kids happy and help us parents fill a night during the holidays, but it was certainly not a legitimate attraction at the time.

The first morning of the marketing retreat, my lifelong friend and fellow counsel, Bill Peel, and I listened to and documented every single thought the family had regarding their business. The entire family was smart and had a lot of insight to offer, but Scott was exceptional. I could tell he had a special gift, and one way or another, this concept was going to be a huge success. By the end of the first day, we determined they had two distinct value propositions: Christmas and Texas. Before we departed at noon the second day, we had identified their target brand: A Texas

Christmas Experience. Strategically putting all of the focus on Santa Claus, we rebranded the concept to Santa's Wonderland: *A Texas Christmas Experience.* We also created the concept of turning Tombstone into Santa's Town, a place that would be a wonderland of food, fun, shopping, and music. Scott was excited about the proposed Tombstone transition and noted, "That will be a really nice value add-on to the light tour."

"Add-on?" I said. "They are going to pay to go into Santa's Town, and we are going to make it worth it. We are also going to upgrade all the lights and double the price of that drive-through ticket as well. You are going to turn this into a holiday destination!"

Scott took off his cowboy hat, scratched his head, and said, "What makes you think someone will pay to go into Santa's Town?" Upon further brainstorming of the town concept, you could see the light come on in Scott's incredibly fertile mind. From that day forward, he locked in on the brand alignment of "A Texas Christmas Experience" and began to roll out his vision.

Knowing we had nailed the direction, it became all about the alignment of the brand assets and, ultimately, execution. If you know the Medlin family, you would never question their ability to execute. Those people flat-out get things done and in a hurry. It doesn't matter whether it is tearing down an old building, putting up a new one, stringing lights, excavating the land, handling the accounting, or whatever. They are multitalented people and, more importantly, passionately committed to their son's dream.

In aligning the assets, it became crystal clear what they needed to do. First, while our firm was busy developing logos, marketing tactics, and the like, Scott and his family would develop Santa's

Town and get it ready the best they could for the next season. Remember, at the time, this was a very small family business, and they did not have big money to throw at the opportunity. To make it financially feasible, they had to do as much of the work themselves as they could.

They started to transform the entire concept immediately. They ordered more lights, began remodeling the buildings in Tombstone, fired the gunfighters, and got sign makers hand-painting various displays. Scott also had the idea of adding a giant kettle corn pot to what would be Santa's Town to sell hot, fresh kettle corn along with some hot chocolate. He had so many ideas he couldn't execute them all for this season, and his vision continued to flourish. They worked hard all the way up to the hour of opening for the season, and it was ready.

I remember going in advance to see Scott and assess what they had accomplished prior to the opening. It was mind-boggling for me to see how much they had achieved and how good it looked compared to the previous year. Disney was not quaking in their boots, but Scott was also not finished. Our walk through the park lasted more than an hour, and Scott talked the entire time. Brimming with excitement, he shared the story of every single board, nail, rope, and snowflake they had created. Additionally, he shared all of the things he was going to start working on the minute they ended the coming season.

I was like, "Dude, take a breath and absorb what you and your family have achieved. Carpe diem, baby!"

I distinctly recall him looking at me and simply saying, "No way, man. This is going to be big!"

Year by year, more beautiful lights went up, and the drive-through displays significantly improved as the characters migrated from ply-wood to mechanical. He expanded Santa's Town, hired a live Santa Claus and his wife, Mrs. Claus, for the kids to sit in their laps and share their wish lists. He quickly turned that into a professionally managed photo op with a full production studio knocking out the prints and digital memories. Within a few seasons, Scott had it look-ing like the quintessential Christmas village we had all envisioned. He also added a giant hay wagon ride through the lights as an option to being in your car. Everything he did was lined up square with one mind space: *A Texas Christmas Experience*. If it did not fit with that alignment, he appropriately would not allow it.

One mind space: A Texas Christmas Experience

Next came live music from Nashville and Texas country bands, expanded food offerings, a petting zoo, the addition of various Christmas-themed shops, animatronics, and brand-aligned charac-ters like Marshall Frostbite, the dancing snowman who is sheriff of Santa's Town. Then came the final key strategic move when Scott decided to close the drive-through for cars, allowing only hay rides and horse-drawn carriage rides through the significantly expanded lights, which, by now, had been replaced with even brighter LEDs. He added massive parking lots, more music venues, campfires all around the property, and additional attractions such as a real snow mountain, train rides, a bucking bull ride, and a giant snow globe, to name a few. There is so much more it would literally take an entire book to explain the whole journey. It is truly an amazing success story that warms the heart of all entrepreneurs.

Santa's Wonderland Today

Twenty-five years later, Scott and his family continue to lead the Christmas Experience business in Texas, consistently drawing more than half a million people a year from all over the country. Santa's Wonderland hires 1,600 part-time seasonal employees, and it now takes every bit of two days to see all it has to offer. Many families come back multiple times during the season just to take it all in. He and his wife, Deb, keep a constant eye on the brand, and nothing gets added to the attraction that is not in full brand alignment with the Texas Christmas Experience. Scott will be the first to tell you that the couple of times in the past he veered even a little off brand, it bit him in the frosty ass.

The fabulous 145-acre-plus Texas Christmas theme park is open annually from late October through New Year's Eve. If you are able to make a holiday journey to Santa's Wonderland, I can promise you will find it in perfect brand alignment. Cocoa made by elves, kettle corn stirred by Mrs. Claus, stores filled with beautiful Texas Christmas gifts and decorations, live country holiday music, and much, much more. You may only go once a year, but you will enjoy a magical experience your family will want to make a Christmas tradition.

And, oh, by the way, did I mention those more than 500,000 annual visitors generate north of $25 million in revenues? Like the title says, "Ho-Ho-Ho!"

POTHOLES HIT: 1

THE OWNER'S FOREST

Brand OFF! Scott and his family hit one big pothole during their early years, and that was simply being too close to what they were doing with the lights. Ironically, these owners were surrounded by trees and *could* see the lights, but not the forest! Focused on what at the time was their main attraction, the drive-through lights, they missed the hidden potential of the other assets already on their property, the old Western buildings.

Brand ON! Once we shifted their focus from Christmas to A Texas Christmas Experience, the whole opportunity made perfect common sense and gave them that one thing to align their brand around. The Medlin family took off with that concept and created a sleigh full of success for the next 25 years and are still going strong.

POWER UP! THE POINT OF ALIGNMENT

A Texas Christmas Experience

MARKET CHER! THE STORY OF TONY CHACHERE'S

The venerable Tony Chachere is a legend. Born in 1905 in Opelousas, Louisiana, he spent 89 years loving the South Louisiana lifestyle of hunting, fishing, and, most of all, cooking. After a successful career in sales, Tony's passion for creating and serving great food drove him to the kitchen. With the encouragement of friends and family, he published his first cookbook in 1972—at age 67—titled, *Tony Chachere's Cajun Country Cookbook*. Its popularity, and especially his recipe for what eventually became the company's flagship product, Tony Chachere's Original Creole Seasoning, launched his journey as a renowned chef. Tony was so talented people ultimately referred to him as the "Ole Master" of fine Cajun cuisine, and in 1995, he became the very first inductee into the Louisiana Chef's Hall of Fame. This is a spicy and inspiring story of how brand alignment helped him and his amazing family create a Cajun food dynasty that has flourished for decades.

Brand OFF! Background

Through the years, Tony Chachere's Original Creole Seasoning had grown to become relatively well-known throughout most of Louisiana and into Southeast Texas. While the Louisiana locals knew the seasoning tasted good sprinkled on just about everything you could think of eating, Texans and other potential expansion market customers understandably identified the brand as a *Cajun spice*, which, in turn, they would only use when cooking Cajun food. At the time, once you left their primary market areas in Louisiana, not many people were cooking Cajun dishes, and if they were, it was not very often. This dilemma of infrequent usage was creating early product maturation and sales stagnation, making expansion of the brand beyond their borders quite difficult. Annual sales were hovering around $6 million but the family had a bigger vision for the culinary treat.

Brand ON! Realigning the Brand

Our firm was brought into Opelousas in the early '90s to review the situation and make marketing and advertising recommendations to grow their seasoning business. They had been running the normal gauntlet of ad agencies, who continued to promote the product as it was without ever really challenging the storied brand itself. I'll never forget being in a conference room of Cajun legends from the Chachere family, listening to their impressive story and trying to get an early grasp of the brand. Every one of them had the rich French Louisiana accent, now called Cajun English by many, which I love. Of course, I was born in Port Arthur, Texas, just across from the Louisiana border, so I was part Cajun myself even though I did not have the accent. It was an interesting all-day meeting and tour of the facility. My team and I were totally immersed in the fanatical passion three generations of family and the entire organization exuded for the product. Moreover, everyone we met had a contagious zest for life that immediately endeared us to their potential.

After spending the day absorbing their vast knowledge and expertise, we had an idea of what might be creating their growth stagnation issues, but knew we needed some specific boots-on-the-ground research to better clarify the challenge. We also had noted that the original cardboard shaker can they sold the product in had not changed much since its inception 20 years earlier. It was a green and white can with a black and white stick figure drawing of Tony in a chef's hat tossing vegetable ingredients up in the air. We had a strong hunch there may be an opportunity to leverage the can due to its somewhat recognizable image after all those years of distribution.

Initial research proved that many households had one of the little green-and-white cans somewhere near the back of their spice cabinet but validated that it was only getting used once or twice a year. This ultimately confirmed the primary challenge for the business was to expand the brand outside the Louisiana borders while increasing usage patterns of the product beyond Cajun food. We had to some-how convince people what Tony himself was always touting, "This stuff is good on everything, Cher!" He would boisterously note how he put it on his eggs in the morning, on his sandwich at lunch, in the gourmet dishes he cooked for dinner, and on his popcorn before he went to bed.

Thinking he might be just a little bit overzealous with his selling of the seasoning, we had to try it for ourselves on things other than

Cajun food. So we did, putting it on more than you can imagine. One of my team members even enjoyed it on ice cream. What we learned is this product transcended culinary cuisines throughout all regional culture categories. It was good on Chinese food, Mexican food, Indian food, Italian food, and yes, most of all, American food. It *was* good on everything. Aha! We have a brand opportunity.

The other issue inhibiting growth was that almost no one could pronounce the name. Especially if you saw the can on your grocer's shelves for the first time and read the label: T O N Y C H A C H E R E' S. Good luck. Go for it. I can't even tell you how many different ways that spelling is pronounced. Yet another branding opportunity.

Last but not least, the black-and-white stick figure of Tony on the can was bothersome. You see, Mr. Tony, as his friends and family would call him, was a bigger-than-life character, and this figure was thin and weak. It needed to be brought to life so the figure could grab your attention and engage you in the same way Mr. Tony would. After all, he stood 6'3", had a gregarious personality, and sold some of the spiciest seasoning on the market. The figure on the can representing him needed to be equally as captivating as the man himself—or at least close. Aha! One more opportunity.

That totaled three opportunities we believed would be critical to realigning the brand. First, it's good on everything; second, how to pronounce the name; and, third, bringing the Mr. Tony character to life. So we went to the proverbial drawing board, and the brainstorming began.

The creative process is an evolution of inspiration founded on preparation. Many times, we would have all the answers before we even returned to our office from the client's. Other times, retreat was required to marinate and incubate thoughts and ideas as they presented themselves to find just the right strategy. This brings me to a great side story on this specific alignment initiative.

The creative process is an evolution of inspiration founded on preparation.

After we had evaluated the research findings, we reached out to the Chachere family and suggested we spend a couple of days in retreat with them to discuss and brainstorm what we had learned. They loved the idea and said they had the perfect place. They told us they would take care of all the arrangements. We were like, "Great, where are we going?" They said Mr. Tony had a fishing and hunting camp in the Atchafalaya Swamp, near Opelousas.

Now I don't know how much you know about swamps in South Louisiana, but you've probably seen the movies. First, you have to get there by a special kind of low-water boat, a swamp canoe known as a pirogue. That in and of itself is a life-changing experience when you begin coming face to face with all the swamp creatures peering at you as you glide stealthily under the low-hanging moss. We are talking serious numbers of alligators, nutria, turtles, frogs, pelicans, insects, spiders, and snakes—lots of snakes. Once we arrived at the camp house, they directed us to put our bags on our respective bunks, all in one giant screened-in room. If I remember correctly, the room slept about 20. Can you imagine 14 or so men all sleeping in one room of bunks in a swamp cabin after a night of Cajun food and beer? Then when night falls in a swamp, it is beyond dark, and you can hear everything that moves, chirps, splashes, or chomps. A swamp is not for the faint of heart.

While a couple of my team members were visibly nervous the entire time we were there, we did have one of the most unique experiences of our lives. As you might imagine, we enjoyed the best food you could ever dream of and all the nighttime stories that come from a cabin full of creatives and lively Cajuns. We later learned this particular swamp cabin was legendary, hosting both dignitaries and regular folks like us from all over the world. Anyone who has made that journey to this gourmet haven counts themselves among the fortunate. We even got a little work done along the way.

Back to the three opportunities. Where was the magic in bringing all of this together to accomplish exponential growth? What was the key to aligning the brand for long-term success? We started where the whole company originally began, with the character of Mr. Tony himself. We took the most visible brand icon they had, the little green-and-white can, and replaced the stick figure with a new cartoon version of Mr. Tony you fall in love with the second you lay eyes on him. We brought the namesake and spirit of the brand to life in the place where he was most visible, on the can.

We also knew we could use this dynamic character across their current line of packaged seasonings, as well as any new products they would be developing in the future. This affable Mr. Tony, affectionately known to us as Little Tony, would carry the fun and spirit of the beloved man and his culinary exploits throughout anything the company would do going forward. Opportunity 3 solved. Mr. Tony would be brought to life on all product offerings.

⚡

One mind space:
A Little Tony on everything

Convinced our beloved Little Tony would be the perfect spokesman for our new television campaign, we developed TV spots to capture Opportunities 1 and 2. Playing off the well-known *Around the World in 80 Days* theme, Little Tony would fly Around the World in 80 Meals in his biplane, stopping to experience the various regional cultural food categories mentioned earlier, and sprinkling Tony Chachere's Original Creole Seasoning on notable cuisines of each region he visited. In every 30-second episode, an announcer in a Don Pardo–like voice would present Little Tony and the country he would be visiting, invariably mispronouncing the name Chachere, tinged with vernacular of that particular country. For Mexican food, it was "Tony Cha-wa-wa's," Chinese food was "Tony Chow-Chi's," and so on. Provoked by this, Little Tony would lean out of his biplane to correct the announcer by emphatically yelling out the proper pronunciation, "Tony Sa'-shur-ees!" The spots closed with the tagline: "Good on Everything. Available Everywhere."

These commercials allowed us to show the seasoning was good on everything while cleverly coaching people on the correct way to pronounce the name several times throughout each spot. We would also highlight the newer version of the Little Green Can everyone had come to love to ensure visible shelf recognition and connection with the product. Opportunities 1 and 2 solved. Sales went up 40% in the first year, and we were well on our way to profitable expansion.

Tony Chachere's Today

That one, two, three punch did the trick, and the brand took off like a scared creative in a swamp camp. A few years later, we were honored to have Mr. Tony fly himself and his entire leadership team to Houston to join us for our firm's 15th Anniversary Rodeo Celebration. A few months later, Mr. Tony would pass at 89 years of age. We loved Mr. Tony, his spitting image son Alex Chachere, who successfully took the company over after Mr. Tony, and his own talented son, Mr. Tony's grandson, Don "Buzzy" Chachere Jr., who took the reins following Alex's retirement from the company in 2000. Buzzy continues to lead the organization today, along with a host of other great team members. They have guided that 50-plus-year-old company to magnificent growth and expansion into markets across the United States, with annual sales topping $100 million. Their product lines now range from marinades to prepared box dinners to frozen foods, all of which boast the lovable Little Tony on them 30 years later. They are a genuine group of caring people and professionals who love nothing more than the smile on customers' faces when they taste good food. The Chacheres are truly one of the greatest families I have ever known and another role model client in keeping a great brand in alignment. "Laissez les bon temps rouler!"

POTHOLES HIT: 1

THE OWNER'S FOREST

Brand OFF! Even though the Chachere family had three opportunities we believed would be critical to realigning the brand, they had still only hit one pothole. When you are focused on flavor and the continued creation of great products under the tutelage of a famous chef, it is easy to become clouded by your own story. Deep in the forest of creating more great Cajun dishes and perfecting the production process, capturing the magic of their main character was not a priority.

Brand ON! When we combined the Little Tony character concept, making fun of the confusion in the name, and the expanded uses of their flagship product, we were able to create a swamp full of opportunity. The Chachere family capitalized on it for the next 25 years, ultimately becoming one of the most recognizable product lines in most any grocery store today.

POWER UP! THE POINT OF ALIGNMENT

A Little Tony on everything!

LIFE CHANGING SMILES:
THE STORY OF DOCTORS IMPLANTS

Our firm was very fortunate to have the unique timing and opportunity to be a key player in creating the healthcare marketing industry. Prior to our foray into that nascent space in the '80s, it was considered unethical for a physician, hospital, or group practice to even consider promoting itself or its services. It was seen as highly unprofessional. We pioneered a basic change in strategic thinking and positioned marketing to provide patients much needed information while helping physicians and hospitals learn to inform the market of their capabilities as opposed to hiding behind a little frosted sliding glass window in a waiting room. This paradigm shift changed the landscape and helped make healthcare marketing the burgeoning industry it is today.

During our time leading our healthcare client decision-makers to better brand alignment initiatives, we encountered a number of prominent physicians and surgeons who were absolutely brilliant people. They were not only extremely smart and very well trained but also blessed with personal gifts God shares only with those He wants serving as His physicians. These were amazing men and women I greatly respect.

Brand OFF! Background

Recently, I had an accomplished oral and maxillofacial surgeon seek me out for advice. He knew of my reputation in the branding world and, in particular, my healthcare expertise as it related directly to his practice. He asked if I would take a look at his current situation and see if there was anything I could do to help them break through the growth stagnation they were experiencing. I was so inclined to say, "Sure, take two aspirin and call me in the morning," but discretion won out, and I listened to his story. I quickly learned this young doc, only 38 years of age, was one of those rare people God chose to share a special gift with in order that he may help others. And help others he does.

Andrew Mueller is a highly specialized, board-certified oral and maxillofacial surgeon who is a master at giving patients their lives back. He specializes in what the market calls *full mouth implants.* Dr. M, as I like to call him, can take the worst set of teeth—and even a lack thereof—and, in one amazing surgery, install the most beautiful, natural smile you could possibly imagine. I would have never believed the degree of perfectionism he achieves with his patients, regardless of their deteriorated bone health, until I witnessed it myself many times over. He is truly magical at what he does, how he does it, and the incredibly high 99% success rate of which he is so rightfully proud.

Dr. M started his practice in 2018 by acquiring another doctor's business in the Wichita Falls, Texas, market. He then created a new primary headquarters in San Antonio, Texas, and another center in Oklahoma City. He was continually adding more top doctors like himself to grow the business in order to meet the massive market demand from the millions of people who need a full set of new teeth.

During this early growth time, Dr. M learned the full mouth implant surgeries were profitable enough he could afford to run local television commercials to get the word out in the small markets where he was located. He hired an ad agency, and they launched TV spots focused on patient testimonials, mirroring the style of commercials run by the two top national full mouth implant providers he considered his competition. It worked for him for a while, and he was able to experience reasonable growth in his practice merely by getting his message out. Then COVID hit, which was quite possibly the best thing to ever happen to him, because everyone had to stay at home and watch TV, driving his number of inquiries through the roof.

This manna from above lasted for about nine months before people began leaving their houses and not seeing as many of his commercials. As would most business owners, Dr. M became addicted to the success, notoriety, and cash flow provided by the media campaign, so he started looking for answers. He personally began tweaking media buys and creative approaches; Dr. M took great pride in figuring things out for himself, and as smart as he is, why not? Simultaneously, he was challenging his in-house marketing team of two people to work with him to find a solution, but it just wasn't happening.

He ultimately decided his internal team did not have the horsepower needed to drive the success levels he wanted to achieve so he set out to hire a CMO (chief marketing officer). He had been led to believe that adding another person, a very expensive employee, was the miracle cure he was seeking. After weeks of searching, he became increasingly frustrated with the process and the search consultant, so he approached me for direction. When we originally met, he still believed hiring the right CMO would cure most of his business development ills. After the first 15 minutes of our discussion, I knew we were onto something very different and significantly bigger than that. I knew hiring a CMO would be a huge mistake and would compound his problems even further. My biggest challenge was going to be to get him to listen. CMOs usually don't work out well for smaller businesses.

My biggest challenge was going to be to get him to listen.

Most doctors truly believe they can solve any problem themselves, even if it is not in their area of expertise. They believe by talking to a few of their physician friends, reading a book or two, and digging around on the internet, it will sufficiently arm them with enough information to run their own branding firm—or, at the very least, resolve all of their own marketing issues. Dr. M was no different from many of the other brilliant doctors I had the honor to represent.

After listening to his story during our initial visit, the first thing I asked him to tell me about was the name of his practice. "Why do you call it *The Marquis Center?*"

"Why do you ask?" he quickly quipped.

"Well, it has absolutely no relevance to what you do. Marquis is a weird word most people never use in the course of any given year, and it's hard to remember, much less spell. It's a very restrictive name, and I don't see any advantages or relevance, so it may be an opportunity for you."

Dr. M replied, "Well, we're not going to change the name. We've been called that since I took the practice over six years ago, and I like Marquis. We have the Marquis Smile in all our TV spots. We have it on our website. It's everywhere. We are not changing the name," he promptly fired back.

Then he left the door slightly open when he said, "You would have to come up with one hell of a case for changing it." Challenge duly noted. I quickly changed subjects, because I already knew we needed to change the name, so why poke that bear? Don't be afraid to make big changes, even change your name if it's not in alignment.

Don't be afraid to change your name if it's not in alignment.

Several of the Top 7 Potholes sprang to mind at this point: *personal pride and success*, the *wrong brand or concept, compromising to please others, internal marketing employees*, and *external marketing vendors*. Through the course of our two-hour meeting, I learned all of these were in play in this scenario. His car was definitely going bump down the road. Please remember what I suggested from the start: Brand alignment is about maximizing your potential. It is about making a good business a great business. Dr. M was doing well, helping others, and making money, but he was light years from where he could be, and inherently, the smart doctor knew it.

Brand alignment is about making a good business a great business.

Brand ON! Realigning the Brand

This business case is what I affectionately term a *target-rich environment*. There was so much to be done to bring Dr. M's practice into brand alignment and truly maximize his opportunities for success. I inherently knew how much change was coming, what it would cost, how long it would take, and, most importantly, what it would achieve. Once again, my biggest challenge was convincing the good doctor to get out of his own way. Remember, he had already built a very well-run, professional practice and was successful by any measure, and his patients loved him!

Most of the time, when clients seek a marketing solution, they think they are looking for some magical creative slogan, campaign, or media buy that will revolutionize the ad world on Madison Avenue. "Just fix our messaging, tweak our graphics, and we are good to go." Occasionally, that is the best response but usually not when it comes to small businesses. It is paramount that alignment is achieved first and foremost, every single time. There are so many reasons this is true, but the primary reason goes back to common sense. If your brand does not make common sense to your customer—or, in this case, to Dr. M's patients—then you are not in alignment and not maximizing your potential. You could be spending thousands—or, in this case, millions—in advertising and not reaping the benefits

Brand ON!

you could garner if your brand was in alignment. You have to do the hard work and be willing to put everything on the table.

In order to bring the practice into alignment, the first thing we did was get Dr. M to call off the dogs and stop the search for a CMO. Besides, I had taken time to visit with his two internal marketing staff and was very impressed. I knew I could work well with them; they were smart, eager, and coachable. Next was to study the market, assess all of the competition in detail, conduct a lot of mystery shopper calls to full mouth implant practices and visit Marquis Center locations so as to put together a total picture of the landscape we were dealing with. In doing so, it became readily apparent that Dr. M ran one of the best physician practices we had ever encountered. His team and his systems were very professional, organized, efficient, and effective. As the final information came in, the big picture started crystallizing, and we began to develop strategies. Once our exhaustive look under the hood was complete, it was time to present our recommendations.

Our first recommendation was—you guessed it—a name change. While this strategy flew directly in the face of what Dr. M originally wanted, we knew it was what he needed. We had learned from the marketplace that his biggest competitors in the space were all pushing speed and price. They were using various gimmicks to try to cut through a market cluttered with information on the best process and type of implants. They were all using patient testimonials on television to draw prospects into their system. It was an absolute sea of sameness. The one thing they were *not* doing was promoting their doctors—and with good reason. They rarely provided a board-certified oral and maxillofacial surgeon to actually do the work. While technically qualified and certainly legal, they had dentists and periodontists doing the predominance of their patient work, because most top oral and maxillofacial surgeons are out running their own private practice and not working for what we lovingly termed *corporate implant factories.*

—————————— ⚡ ——————————

Don't swim in a sea of sameness.

—————————————————————

I don't know about you, but if I were having all my teeth pulled from my skull and replaced with a brand new mouth designed on the premises, I would seek out the very best surgeon in the business. Dr. M's patients are no different, and the vast majority of the market feels the exact same way. After studying the different marketers of this service, most people ultimately learn that a full mouth implant procedure is expensive and that the legitimate providers all charge about the same amount. At the end of their fact-finding mission, patients usually want the very best surgeon they can find digging around in their face, and I don't blame them.

Since The Marquis Center only used board-certified oral and maxillofacial surgeons to work on their patients, we decided it was mission critical to put their doctors up front. They were already operating that way, so why not be genuine with their market communications and brand themselves as such? Why not be the only ones on TV advocating their best-in-class surgeons, as well as the other highly trained physicians Marquis had in their practice designing smiles and other important technical work? Why not own the strategy of being Doctor Driven!

One mind space: Doctor Driven!

Now take *Doctor Driven!* to the name change. We will never win a creative award for our solution, but we may well be honored someday with the Brilliant but Boring, Perfect Practice Brand Alignment Strategy Award. We renamed the practice Doctors Implants, developed a highly professional medical graphics approach, and positioned the business to be doctor driven in everything it does. Everything. That is the essence of alignment. Everything must be in alignment and make common sense, not just to the internal team but to every patient.

When the TV ads were created, our doctors were the focus, each wearing white lab coats and coming from a place of distinction and professionalism. Then there were smiling patients sprinkled throughout—real ones with fabulous new smiles but all focused on talking about the doctors, not as much about themselves. It is ultimately the doctors the patients are entrusting, not other patients. Moreover, patients take great pride in seeing their doctors on TV, where they can share with their friends, "That's my doc. He did my smile." This pride drives referrals at hyper speed and creates a special camaraderie around the practice and its patient base that spills out into the marketplace.

To learn everything we ultimately strategized, created, and orchestrated for Dr. Mueller's practice to bring it into alignment, you will have to read the book I hope he writes one day. Thanks to his two internal marketing people, Niko and Caroline, the development and implementation of our brand alignment strategy were flawless. They are the rare internal marketing team you want to take to dinner.

Doctors Implants Today

The results were astounding. The inbound calls from the TV and radio were more than double the practice had ever experienced. The close ratio of calls to patients increased, and the monthly case load and revenues skyrocketed. The initial fears about changing the name all disappeared in a matter of days when patients and prospective patients shared comments about wanting the best possible doctor handling their smiles. Moreover, no one was calling the switchboard or asking their doctor if they were still the same Marquis or why they had to change their name. It was all so seamless that we knew it was meant to be. It was all about aligning the one thing that made them great.

It was all about aligning the one thing that made them great.

Dr. Mueller and his family (I didn't mention his mom and dad work for him and fill critical administrative roles in the practice) are special people who know how to get things done. They are sharp, professional, and caring people who are meticulous about their business. They draw immense joy from improving the lives of others, whether it be a smiling new patient or one of their essential team members. The only challenge they face today is finding more top board-certified oral and maxillofacial surgeons to serve the booming markets we all created together.

POTHOLES HIT: 5

WRONG BRAND OR CONCEPT

Brand OFF! The Marquis Center name was a big hurdle they couldn't see. Not only was the name irrelevant to their medical practice, but Marquis is one of those strange words most people never use. It's a hard word to remember, challenging for many to spell, and very restrictive.

Brand ON! Changing the name to Doctors Implants to align with the professional medical brand we were creating was magical. The name now portrays a strong sense of professionalism and credibility for the doctors who were the critical alignment factor in this business.

PERSONAL PRIDE AND SUCCESS

Brand OFF! Dr. M had a lot on his plate and was busy making good money and growing his practice, all while performing several surgeries a day. How was he to be aware of his brand alignment opportunities among all his success?

Brand ON! Dr. M inherently knew there was a wealth of untapped opportunity for his growing practice but was not quite sure how to shine a light on it. Starting with his own self-assessment, then bringing in professionals was the correct solution in this situation.

INTERNAL MARKETING EMPLOYEES

Brand OFF! While Marquis Centers had a talented duo in their marketing department, remember that marketing is not brand alignment. They did not have the experience to know what to look for. Even if they did, it would have been difficult for them to tell a successful surgeon exactly what's wrong when their paycheck depends on him liking their advice.

Brand ON! Bringing in experienced counsel to the internal team while mentoring them along the way allowed Dr. M to make the most of the assets he already had in-house.

EXTERNAL MARKETING VENDORS

Brand OFF! They had major issues in this pothole, one with the original outside marketing firm who gave them the Marquis Centers name and the other with a media salesperson who was leading them down the wrong strategic path. Both had good intentions, but neither had an understanding of the brand.

Brand ON! Once he had a clearer understanding of the impact they were having on his practice, Dr. M was able to make those changes in direction.

THE OWNER'S FOREST

Brand OFF! Dr. M did what he knew best. Between surgeries and growing his practice, he spent a lot of personal time doing research in an attempt to maximize his potential. He was trying to understand the many nuances of branding and marketing, all along not realizing the hidden powers of brand alignment and its benefits.

Brand ON! Dr. M ultimately got out from among all those trees, brought in some outside eyes to help him see the forest, then pulled it all together through an alignment initiative. Today, Doctors Implants continues to break growth records and create life-changing smiles.

POWER UP! THE POINT OF ALIGNMENT

Doctor Driven!

THE AGGIE NETWORK: THE STORY OF THE ASSOCIATION

Not all universities enjoy the fanatical alumni spirit Texas A&M University does. Regardless of that undaunted spirit, making college alums feel like part of something relevant after they graduate and leave campus is a challenge for all school alumni organizations. Compelling them to consistently make financial contributions to the organization is even tougher. This is an inspiring story of a brand that has successfully orchestrated perfect alignment for 25 years while achieving record growth and contributions.

Brand OFF! Background

The Association of Former Students is the 501(c)(3) organization responsible for raising and allocating funding from Texas A&M's more than 575,000 alumnus base. Their stated claim is to exist to strengthen The Association of Former Students, promote the interests and welfare of Texas A&M University, perpetuate the ties of affection and esteem formed in an Aggie's university or college days, and to serve the current student body. I have personal knowledge that they are successful at accomplishing all of that, while consistently ranking in the nation's top public university alumni associations for participation and contribution.

In existence since 1879, The Association is actually only one of several prominent organizations reaching out to Texas A&M's graduates for involvement and investment. The other major entities cultivating the crop are the Texas A&M Foundation, the primary academic fundraising institution for Texas A&M, charged with raising and managing major gift endowments and the group many of you would call their booster club, and the 12th Man Foundation, which represents the schools' athletic interests. Then you have each of the 16 individual colleges within the main campus and a score of special interest organizations, who all tap into the vast resource Aggies fondly call Former Students. This complicated web of outreach without overreach is a complex dance the leaders of these organizations mindfully and strategically navigate on a daily basis. For the sake of this book, this story is only about The Association of Former Students.

It would make sense, especially back in the day, for any alumni association to target its major prospective donors with the predominance of their attention. It is, in fact, how most of them have functioned throughout history. Since the 80/20 theory was normally in play at these philanthropic groups (80% of the money is given by 20% of its donors), it only made good business sense to operate in such a manner. Prior to the turn of the century, most public university alumni groups were grateful to experience anywhere from 2% to 5% participation from their total graduate pool, and out of that small percentage, the

80/20 theory (as much as 90/10 with some) would actually write a check. The Association of Former Students was no different, so we were engaged by the board of directors and their executive director, Randy Matson, to study the landscape and see if there might be a strategy for improving these metrics. They knew Aggies were fervent about their school but were curious as to why such a small percentage of graduates, only 2% at the time, made financial commitments. Why was such a fanatical alumni base not feeling a stronger sense of connection and commitment?

Brand ON! Realigning the Brand

Websites were in their infancy, and there was no social media at that time, so most of the organization's communication to its perspective market was via its glossy alumni magazine *The Texas Aggie*, direct mail, or staged social events. Most graduates got the magazine upon graduation, and if not, you could find one lying around on most any coffee table. If you had any sort of desire to keep in touch with the university after you graduated, *The Texas Aggie* was the go-to source. The publication ultimately carried the heavy load of message dissemination for the organization.

The magazine had a look of authority to it. It was well produced and included up-to-date information alumni would want to know about the initiatives and events going on at Texas A&M. It included special interest stories about the school, various graduates, A&M clubs around the world, Aggie babies born, and even a section called Silver Taps honoring those Aggies who had passed before us. It was widely read and had everything an alum could want.

Brand ON!

For some odd nostalgic reason, I had saved every issue of the publication since I had graduated in 1978. I wanted to be like those successful graduates they wrote about, and I also wanted to make a difference in the future of our school and the lives of all those who would pass through its doors in the future. After interviewing all the leaders at The Association, my team and I laid every single one of these magazines out in a mosaic format on the floor so we could view the covers all at once. Remember, they weren't designed on computers at the time, so there was no scrolling through digital images on the screen. As we'd anticipated, the collective covers told a story. The story was one of the Aggie spirit and our graduates' unyielding sacrifice and commitment to unselfishly give everything they could to our alma mater's ultimate success. Then the obvious came to light.

It became apparent that most every cover story or inside lead story was about a big-name Aggie grad who had just made a monstrous financial gift. It was certainly understandable why that was the rhythm of the piece, and someone giving millions absolutely deserved to be featured on the cover. What they didn't realize was the overall message it was projecting over time and the brand image that was being crafted in the minds of young graduates. While it was never intentional, the message being broadcast was "We really care a lot about Former Students who can give us a lot of money!" In its simplest form, it said, "We aren't too excited about those smaller gifts."

One of the issues featured a man who had graciously donated an island in Guam, and while that was totally worthy of celebration, I thought to myself, "One day, when I own an island, I am going to give it to Texas A&M, but until then, I don't matter." Was the network of Aggies, my fellow graduates, only interested in the multimillion-dollar gifts? Would my $50 matter? Was I not part of The Association of Former Students until my contributions were more significant? Would I ever be able to give enough to matter?

Our team quickly realized this could be an issue and began talking to other graduates. We were spot-on. People did not feel like their gifts mattered until they had significantly more zeros on the end, so they just checked out altogether. They felt like they weren't relevant and disengaged from being an active participant. Sure, they would still make small gifts to the 12th Man Foundation so they could get tickets to the football games, but they planted the "I'll make a difference giving to The Association someday in the future" seed in the distant corridors of their minds. This led to an unintended elitist image that you had to be old and rich to matter.

What The Association leadership had not realized was the unique growth of the graduate base in conjunction with the "smaller gifts don't matter" messaging. One of the poignant facts we learned at that time was that over half of the alums of Texas A&M had graduated since 1980. Think about it: The school started in 1876, yet due to its significant popularity and growth, over half the graduates at the time we led the project had only been out of school in the last 20 years. That meant a multitude of graduates at that time were still very new in the workforce and trying to find their way to pay bills, not make major donations to their school. Yet the focus of communications had unintentionally been on graduate classes from 30–50 years out of school who were writing the bigger checks. They were also unintentionally leaving out the $50 donor, who, by way of feeling engaged early after graduation, would be groomed into that Aggie who is then conditioned to make that major endowment contribution at a later time.

The alignment challenge became crystal clear. We had to find a way to make sure every single A&M graduate knew their gift, regardless of size, mattered. Graduates all wore the same special Aggie Ring, so why shouldn't they all be a part of The Association of Former Students? The organization could no longer unintentionally dismiss smaller gifts and, therefore, participation. Any good philanthropic fundraiser will tell you participation is the first step to getting a donor to make a gift. Involvement is key, because it follows the heart, and the checkbook follows the involvement.

At the time, the Aggie network of graduates was something people occasionally talked and even joked about. It was almost as if it were a secret cult. It wasn't, but Aggies were intensely loyal to each other and stuck together through thick and thin. Aggies hired Aggies. Aggies were always there for Aggies. While this network of graduates was gossiped about, it was never owned in name. No one ever had the idea of bringing the actual nomenclature forward, branding it and owning it. We did.

One mind space: The Aggie Network

The timing was perfect, so we made the recommendation for The Association of Former Students to own *The Aggie Network* as a brand, to be represented by an artistic rendition of the famed Aggie

Ring revered by all graduates. The next step was to communicate, through the *Texas Aggie* magazine and other media channels that *everyone* was part of the Aggie Network. We did so with an internal campaign titled "The Ring Is the Thing." It featured graduates from all walks of life, all ages, all races, and donors of all sizes, sporting their Aggie Ring. It brought forth the image that we are all Aggies and that we are all part of the Aggie Network and that we can all make a difference with gifts and involvement at all levels. This was one instance where using pride as an attractor was highly successful. It was an absolute home run, and I can tell you many personal stories that resulted from the power of this initiative. Anecdotes we could have never imagined sprang forth by opening up the legitimate value of everyone's contribution.

The Association Today

My favorite part of this success story is not how we found the hidden potential, created the magic, brought the organization's brand into alignment, and led a hugely successful launch. The very best and most important part of this story is how the leadership at The Association not only embraced the brand but has meticulously kept the wheels in alignment and tires balanced all the way down the road for 25 successful years. This has resulted in a growth to 11% participation and contributions upward of $13 million per year, all while the graduate population has grown to 600,000+.

The Texas Aggie is still in existence but, as you might imagine, is no longer the main conduit of communication. The Association marketing team has artfully developed the AggieNetwork.com website and created more effective social media extensions than you can imagine. They host events everywhere around campus and around the globe. They are constantly reaching out to graduates in a number of creative ways that all align with the brand. And I dare you to find a piece of communication or signage that does not in some form or fashion include the artistic replica or the Aggie Ring we created in 1998 to represent the Aggie Network. Consistency matters in brand alignment, and it's hard to deliver year after year. These people make it happen.

Consistency matters in brand alignment, and it's hard to deliver year after year.

All the credit here goes to their leader for the past 25 years, Porter Garner, The Association CEO; his team; and the various rotating members of the Association of Former Students Board of Directors who empower them to do their job. This group of people committed on day one to never stray from the brand, and as enticing as it is at times to change for the sake of change, they have not. They have remained loyal to the authenticity and style of the brand and leveraged it in more creative ways than I can count. In fact, I often share this story as the single most perfect example I have ever witnessed of a large organization staying true to a brand and maximizing its impact over time. The Association is an absolute role model for brand alignment success from a non-profit service organization. Gig 'em!

POTHOLES HIT: 3

THE OWNER'S FOREST

Brand OFF! It is always a challenge for a large nonprofit to see outside beyond its own trees due to the varied constituencies it serves. The Association was taking care of their bigger donors, as they should, and was unaware of how it was making others feel irrelevant. That approach was also taking a big toll on future major donors who grow from current smaller donors when their careers advance.

Brand ON! Helping The Association leadership shine a light on this opportunity to be more inclusive in their approach, while still honoring their biggest donors, changed everything.

COMPROMISING TO PLEASE OTHERS

Brand OFF! As I noted above, nonprofits face big obstacles when it comes to pleasing all of their various constituencies, especially when many of them are big donors themselves. Everyone has an opinion, and while you need to consider those opinions, remember that group branding usually leads to mediocrity. Funny note: One director on the board said before we began the project, "Over my dead body are you going to change our logo!" Boom.

Brand ON! Nonprofits generally have a bigger challenge in this pothole, because their decision-makers are usually significant donors. This complicates the landscape, but at some point, someone needs to step forward and lead if you are going to get your brand in alignment.

PERSONAL PRIDE AND SUCCESS

Brand OFF! For this one, we need to rename it *school pride and success*. Texas A&M has a strong sense of tradition, and sometimes that means getting out of our own way when change is important. Thankfully, great leaders have improved this culture, and The Association of Former Students has been a lead organization for the university in this regard.

Brand ON! Great brand alignment requires strong leadership, which quite often means flying in the face of tradition. Embracing and realigning the pride paid off in spades in this story.

POWER UP! THE POINT OF ALIGNMENT

The Aggie Network

LIFE IN THE FAST LANE: THE STORY OF SAFEWAY DRIVING

Granted, driver's education schools are not a very exciting business, until you consider the fact that every time you and your loved ones get into a car could be your last. Now I have your attention.

Brand OFF! Background

Back in the '70s, driver's education was pretty much taught by your local high school coaches, doubling as part-time driving professionals. Coach Gene Walker was one of those coaches, but he became the exception. Originally teaching driver's ed to high school kids as a side gig to supplement his football coaching salary, Coach Walker and his wife, Jeanne, decided it was time to get serious about the business. He left coaching, and they founded SafeWay Driving in 1973 to fuel their passion for developing well-prepared young drivers while trying to carve out a living for their family. Originally named Spring Branch Driving Schools, they embarked on a journey for nearly four decades that grew into five locations across the Greater Houston area and impacted the lives of thousands of people.

Coach Walker coached with my father, who was the high school basketball coach at the same school, Memorial Senior High in Houston. He originally tried to get my father to join him full time, but dad decided to stick solely to coaching, relegating his driver training purely to part-time efforts. Thirty-seven years later, I learned Coach Walker was putting together a prospectus for selling his business so he and Jeanne could retire and spend more time with the grandkids. To make a really long story short, he asked me to take a look at the package, and in 2010, we made an investment to buy the company. We saw an opportunity not only to help an old family friend but to take a solid small business with absolutely horrible brand alignment into a whole new world.

Moreover, we all believed we could help transform an antiquated but very important industry. At the time, most every company in the driver's education business was providing driver training services based on an 80-year-old business model: Classrooms, lots of paper, old used cars, and competing by being the lowest price provider was the standard across the competitive landscape. Everyone involved knew we had the chance to do something big and make a positive impact on thousands of lives. Knowing this particular rebranding initiative would take the better part of 18 months, as well as a significant commitment of resources, I buckled up for the ride just as I had for my clients so many times before.

Brand ON! Realigning the Brand

The reason everyone in the industry was missing the opportunity was simple. Getting a driver's license was a state requirement designed for teenagers who only had to meet the state-mandated minimums and nothing more, thereby ensuring their driver's license but not necessarily their safety. This didn't provide much value and meant that all driving schools, including SafeWay, were a very-low-to-no-profit-margin business. Everyone in the industry had historically offered the absolute minimum number of hours required to obtain a license. So many hours in the classroom and so many hours behind the wheel of the car with an instructor, and you're done. No one ever focused on what it actually took to train someone to be a safe driver. The industry was totally fixated on the minimum it took to help a student pass the driver's test. That's how they marketed, how they set their pricing, and how they performed: the bare minimum.

It is why Coach had a $2 million business only taking home around $150,000 or so per year for all those efforts. It's why he paid his instructors low wages. It's why he scoured the classified ads every day to see who was selling an old junker car he could purchase and install a passenger-side brake to make into a cheap driver's ed car. It's why his cars were all different colors, most with hues of rust and some with holes in the floorboard. When I asked him about it, he said, "Everyone operates this way. They don't have a choice." This was incredibly painful for me to witness but was giving me a clear picture of the industry mentality and reminding me that the owners of most of these businesses were old coaches, teachers, and driver's ed trainers, not business school grads.

We chose to take the high road and essentially adopted the internal attitude of "Do you just want your child to get a license, or do you want them to learn how to drive?" We asked our 60-plus driving instructors on staff at the time to answer the following question: "If it were your teenage child, how many hours of behind-the-wheel training would you require to make them a safe driver?" At the time, the State of Texas requirement was seven hours. Our staff of highly trained professional driving instructors unanimously agreed on 27 hours minimum behind the wheel. That makes for a huge training difference between getting a license and learning how to drive.

With that knowledge, we set forth to transform the industry. To do so, we first transformed ourselves by committing to our *one thing*; our stated purpose was "preventing the phone call nobody wants." We knew if we could align everything we did around that purpose, we could save lives, reinvigorate an industry, and make some good money along the way.

One mind space: Preventing the phone call nobody wants

Our primary initiative was to work with State of Texas education leadership and the industry to help change a law, allowing online lessons to replace the classroom portion of driver training. The classroom was more of a basic introduction to rules of the road and driving nomenclature we knew could be easily taught online, preventing the need for expensive classrooms and parents having to make two trips a day to the school for their teen. We were ultimately successful at achieving this initiative.

Next, we increased prices and began offering packages with significantly more hours of in-car driver training than were required by the state, which also increased our students' time behind the wheel and, therefore, their safety on the road. This immediately began saving lives and boosting profit margins to levels never before seen in the industry. It also gave concerned parents a peace of mind that was the primary brand alignment key we were after, since they wrote the check.

We were obviously making a lot of good noise early in the business, because I was asked to be a keynote speaker at the Driving School Association of the Americas' annual conference just a year into taking over SafeWay. With my brand leadership and marketing background, I thought I could provide the audience of 200 driving school owners some valuable insight into the industry that they had never heard before. I felt like I could give them a glimpse into the future and was willing to share with them what we had learned and the direction we were going. I genuinely wanted them to take this knowledge home and put it to use. I presented the case for more hours of behind-the-wheel training. I shed light on how truly valuable a life-saving service they were providing and why they should be charging more money. I even shared exactly what we had started charging months earlier and the incredibly positive impact it had on our bottom line. I showed them how we could pay our professional instructors a lot more than they were paying theirs. I showed them how we purchased nothing but new cars for our training students to drive. To say I laid the strategy in their laps would be the understatement of all understatements.

There was a sizable line of people waiting to talk to me following my speech, and I thought, *OMG, here come the accolades and adoration.* Wrong. Most of them waited in line to tell me I was nuts.

The very first guy said, "Thank you for your inspiring speech, Mr. Coleman, but you won't be here next year because you will be out of business. You are crazy if you think parents are going to pay more for their teen's driver training when they are not required to do so. I appreciate your time, and you're a good speaker, but you don't know anything about running a driving school." Ouch. And the feedback pretty much stayed along those lines of predicted failure, including follow-up calls and even a letter wishing me the best and asking if I would call them when we closed our doors so they could buy our cars. Jeez. Tough crowd.

Regardless of the myriad of warnings, we continued implementation of our new brand alignment strategies. We rebranded all of our retail classroom locations with a new roadway themed look and logo. The look was an asphalt gray offset by accents of caution-sign yellow, vibrant red, and polar white, with touches of black. The logo was a diamond-shaped yellow caution sign with *SafeWay Driving* in the center, outlined in black. We aligned all of the interiors and signage to match and made sure every item that entered those doors fit the brand. We shot new videos for all of the training segments and integrated them throughout our presentations and teaching systems. We took Coach Walker's nationally acclaimed curriculum and modernized it to match the brand while keeping the essence of his touch throughout the process.

To complete the alignment, we ordered 40 brand-new white Toyota Corollas. I will never forget the look on Coach's face when he saw those shiny new wheels begin rolling into the parking lot.

He said, "Coleman, how do you think you can afford all-new vehicles like that?"

I responded by saying, "Coach, we can't afford not to buy them. Toyota is currently offering a 0% interest deal, and after running some financial analysis, we learned our monthly payments will actually be $50 less per car than you were paying to own and maintain those clunkers, because all of our repairs and maintenance are free for five years. Not to mention we don't have to spend time going through the classifieds and driving out to evaluate and purchase old cars."

He smiled that special smile only Coach Walker can. We fully branded the cars with dynamic new SafeWay Driving graphics, and they literally became rolling billboards that generated more incoming sales calls and brand pride than you can imagine. Funny, but the competitors only had small magnetic signs on their cars that said *Drivers Ed* until a year or so later, when we began noticing several of their cars on the streets fully branded with their company names. Ah, imitation—the sincerest form of flattery.

The next step was the development of integrated online processes and a digital online learning management system to more efficiently and effectively onboard and train instructors and team members. By now, we were training a record number of students, and profitability had quadrupled. Soon after, we completed the digital transformation process and took the business fully paperless. This was all in preparation for the creation, documentation, and repositioning of the company to ultimately become a successful franchisor organization. We wanted entrepreneurs around the state—and, ultimately, around the country—to be able to bring the very best in driver training to their neighborhoods. We were confident our totally integrated digital systems, acclaimed modern curriculum, and well-aligned brand would allow them to be successful franchisees by following our precisely defined model. We had uncovered the hidden power of our brand alignment and wanted to share it with other like-minded owners.

During our final preparation to franchise, a private equity group approached us to buy controlling interest in the business, and we were off to the races. In our first year of franchising, we successfully awarded 16 franchises to some great people, and word got out fast about what we were doing at SafeWay. My job was complete when I exited the company so investors could hire new leadership to take the company into the future.

SafeWay Driving Today

To this day, SafeWay Driving continues its mission to prevent the phone call nobody wants. The equity investors did their deal, hit most all of the potholes along the way, then sold the business back nearly a decade later to one of our original owners, former NASCAR driver and my son, Brad Coleman. He and our first franchisee, Rick Nussle, have teamed up to lead the business to new heights. They are bringing things back into alignment as the car had gotten a bit off course. Let's just say the wheels were wobbling terribly, and the tires were about to blow.

That can happen to any organization when the leaders consistently hit the potholes. Now the new owners are once again setting records and offering the very best in personalized driver training to adult, corporate, and teen drivers. More impressive to me, however, is their continued unwavering commitment to driver safety. They take it very seriously, which is what every parent should want for their child and every company for their driver employees.

Thanks to Brad and Rick, SafeWay Driving now has over 50 years of success and totals more than 275,000 trained drivers. It is no wonder the founder, Coach Walker, is a nationally respected authority and pioneer in the driver education and training industry. He was instrumental in creating how driver's education was taught—and still is today. I can personally share with you it was quite an honor to work with Coach throughout the SafeWay Driving acquisition and brand realignment process. He and Jeanne are two of the world's greatest people and will forever have my love and gratitude.

POTHOLES HIT: 2

COMPROMISING TO PLEASE OTHERS

Brand OFF! The compromise in this instance was with the marketplace to try and please who they thought was the end user. They assumed parents wanted the cheapest driver's education for their child just to get past the states' minimum requirement. The entire industry was involved in this mass compromise, and no one was willing to budge. This created stagnation, low margins, and poor-quality instruction at many training centers.

Brand ON! As you read, we blew this wide open and changed the narrative to parents wanting what's best for their children, not necessarily what's cheapest. This changed an industry.

THE OWNER'S FOREST

Brand OFF! It's really hard to see the forest through all of the trees you have planted over 40 years. Coach and Jeanne were so entrenched in those trees that they could not see the big-picture opportunity that was eluding them.

Brand ON! We cultivated the great trees they had planted by realigning most every one of them to the new reality of the marketplace we were creating. It not only changed an industry but significantly enhanced operations, the quality of instruction, and profitability. Years later, Brad and Rick keep making all the necessary adjustments along the road to extend the aligned brand for continued success while saving countless lives.

POWER UP! THE POINT OF ALIGNMENT

Preventing the phone call nobody wants

Chance Collar Company

TAKE A CHANCE: THE STORY OF CHANCE COLLAR COMPANY

Thanks in advance for allowing me to tell you this really old story. Sure, it's dated, but there is something to learn from it; it's fun, and it includes the Eighth Wonder of the World. I share this snippet from my early career only to illustrate how even in a down-and-dirty, industrial manufacturing business like producing spiral weight drill pipe for drilling rigs, you can still find that key alignment point and leverage your *one thing* into total brand alignment success.

Brand OFF! Background

What are the odds? The man who gave me my chance was named Glenn Chance. He and his friends Jim Hall and Dick Cox ran an oil field drill pipe manufacturing company out of an office trailer in Pearland, Texas, in 1980. They were one of my first clients at the ripe old age of 24, but they were also the men who saw something in me, put their money down on the table, and said, "Go start your own marketing firm, and pay us back when you make it."

In the early '80s, there was an oil glut, with a significant surplus of crude oil caused by reduced demand following the oil crisis of the '70s. The result was a six-year decline in the price of oil, reducing the per barrel price in half by 1986, but drilling was skyrocketing for non-OPEC countries. This meant there was a strong demand for drilling and production-related products in and from the United States. The predominance of these oil field manufacturing and service companies were located in Texas, Louisiana, and Oklahoma.

Brand alignment was not even a thing at the time. Sales and marketing programs consisted of large quantities of Crown Royal, hunting and fishing trips, barbecues, crawfish boils, company logos on baseball caps, and various other activities used to entice prospective buyers. Very few companies had an internal marketing director, and most advertising was accomplished through buying space in the four major industry trade journals. These were all legitimate publications that covered various aspects of the world oil business, each specializing in various segments of the industry. The publications' sales reps would call on these small oil field companies, convince them to buy ads, then help them put the graphics together. Pretty rustic until a few select ad agencies, ours being one of them, got involved in the business and began to up the quality of the game.

Also integrated into most every company's loosely written marketing plan was attendance at various industry trade shows hosted around the country. Almost everyone in the industry would come to these four-day extravaganzas where new products, engineering, and technology were on display for visitors to learn and, hopefully, upon returning home, write purchase orders. In the '80s, trade show display booths ranged from an introductory 10 × 10-foot space to immeasurable, custom monstrosities appearing as big as a city block, featuring items such as full-size trucks and drilling rig platforms. Extravagant custom booths were planned and built a year in advance. Product displays were created, sales materials produced, and teams of people trained, including professional models to promote the company's various products and services. There was no end to the creativity—or money—expended in an attempt to be the talk of the show for that particular year in a relentless effort to draw throngs of guests to your booth.

The granddaddy of them all was the OTC, which stands for Offshore Technology Conference. It was held annually in Houston, at the Astrodome, the "Eighth Wonder of the World." The display space included the Astrohall and the Astro Arena, now collectively known as NRG Park. It also included the entire complex parking lot in order for those companies whose products would not fit into the indoor venues to display their giant trucks, drilling rigs, huge valves, and so on for prospective buyers to see. It was quite a major event for the city of Houston and for the industry, drawing well over 100,000 industry-qualified visitors. It still runs today as one of the premiere trade meetings in the world.

In 1981, we had three clients committed to participating in the OTC, pledging budgets from $20,000 to $200,000 for the four-day extravaganza. The big budget happened to be Chance Collar Company, who was introducing a brand-new line of spiral weight drill pipe that year, and the leaders wanted to make a huge splash. "Spare no expense and let 'er rip!" quipped Mr. Chance.

While that was incredibly inspiring, I also knew it was a boundaryless challenge to ensure they were the talk of the show. These guys had just invested their money in me to start my firm and were counting on me to garner the highest marketing accolades in the industry by dominating that show with their very first entrée into the fray. While I was pumped, I was also feeling the pressure. Where in the world would we start, and what was exciting or noteworthy about a bunch of 30-foot strands of spiraled, weighted pipe? How would we differentiate them from the other pipe manufacturers and draw scores of visitors to their particular display, where the sales team could get quality time with prospects? How would we generate the level of interest and results our client was after? How would we make Mr. Chance proud?

Brand ON! Realigning the Brand

Timing is everything, right? Second to brand alignment, I agree. I got my team, as small and embryonic as it was, in front of a whiteboard and started identifying our client's advantages and differentiators. It was a very short list. Ultimately, the one unique value proposition we had was their distinctive name, *Chance* Collar Company. We had to find ways to put the Chance name at the center of our brand alignment strategy and extend it through all of our activation plans. After that revelation, we also had to find ways to make it relevant.

One mind space: Intentionally capitalize on the unique name Chance

---

We started listing what was going on in the world at that time. What was hot in the media and creating a lot of noise on existing media channels? Well, let's see. *Urban Cowboy*, starring John Travolta, was filmed in Houston and had been released six months prior. It was definitely the hottest thing going. Oh yeah, and so was the mechanical bull, the kind they used solely for training rodeo bull riders, which caused a big stir in the movie and was creating all kinds of press and excitement. Don't forget, people come to OTC from all over the world to visit Texas, cameras around their neck, hoping to see a few cowboys.

"I got it!" Being an avid country and western fan, I was taking in all the honky-tonks on the weekends, so the timing for my idea was serendipitous. "Let's capture the excitement around *Urban Cowboy*, the Gilley's honky-tonk, and the mechanical bull from the movie. Let's get all these foreign visitors amped up about seeing real Texas cowboys." Then we thought, let's get John Travolta into our booth! Nah, how about another cowboy star, someone a little more cowboy? How about Larry Hagman, J.R. from CBS's TV mega-hit *Dallas*? That was the number one TV show at the time and had an obvious Texas theme. Well, old J.R. wanted way too much money to make an appearance. A brand-new TV show had just launched two months earlier on ABC to compete with *Dallas*, called *Dynasty*. It was created by Richard and Esther Shapiro and produced by Aaron Spelling and was coming after *Dallas*. More importantly, *Dynasty* was about the trials and tribulations of an oil field family named the Carringtons. Perfect. One of the show's stars was Dale Robertson, who played Walter Lankershim, an oil field wildcatter. Perfect. Dale was a childhood idol of mine from the days he drove the stagecoach in the *Tales of Wells Fargo*. He was a rough and tough, devilishly handsome cowboy who would fit in very well with our crowd.

When reaching out to try and hire Dale, I was told our agent would have to fly to his ranch just outside of Oklahoma City and tell him in person exactly what the gig would look like and why we wanted him involved. "Agent my ass!" I said. "I will personally get on that plane to go explain this opportunity to Mr. Robertson." A selfish play perhaps, but worst-case scenario, I would get to meet one of my childhood cowboy heroes. So hat in hand and boots on feet, I got on the plane, flew to Oklahoma City, got in the rental car, and headed for Yukon, Oklahoma, where Dale's ranch was located.

It was so cool. When I pulled up to the front of the sprawling house, the actual Wells Fargo strongbox off the stagecoach was sitting right there on the front porch. I immediately had huge flashbacks from my six-year-old days wearing my toy holster, chaps, and cowboy hat and watching Dale drive that stagecoach through Indian country. Am I really standing here about to meet Dale Robertson? Then a really pretty lady came to the door and said, "You must be Mr. Coleman."

I nervously respond, "Y-y-y-y-y-y-y-e-e-e-s-s-s-s-s-m-a-a-a-a-a-m."

She said, "Mr. Robertson is in the den waiting for you."

I damn near pooped in my pants.

Dale was even more striking in person than he was on the silver screen. He was incredibly friendly right off the bat. He starts out, "Let's saddle up and go for a ride." Then I did mess my pants. I am about to go ride the range with a cowboy hero of my childhood? Who the hell gets to do that? I was beside myself. We went outside, walked toward the barn, and passed a golf cart. Dale said, "Get in," while pointing to the passenger seat of the golf cart. Damn. No horse for me. Oh well, still a major thrill. We rode his ranch for half an hour while he dictated orders into his handheld tape recorder. Upon returning to the house, he took the mini tape out and tossed it on his assistant's desk and said, "Tell the boys they got a busy day ahead, and let me know when it's all done."

He turned to me and said, "Now tell me about you."

Where do I start? What do I share? I have no story like Dale's. The truth just flowed, and it all worked out.

Then he says, "I like you. So, tell me about your idea."

I shared my idea and how much it would mean to me and my client to have him join us in Houston to represent Chance Collar Company at the OTC in a few months. He looked me in the eye and said, "Let's do it." Again, my pants.

All right, back to brand alignment. Granted, the concept was taking shape. Here it is: We build a small Western town in the parking lot of the Astrodome. We make it a full-size saloon, flanked by a corral and totally surrounded by wooden ranch-style fencing. The saloon was to include a hidden sideway door with a conference room behind it. Exhibitors were not actually supposed to sell products out of their booths, so we were just taking orders and secretly closing deals. A saloon girl would greet our guests, fully attired in authentic Western garb, pour them a drink, and show them the hidden door of the conference room. But this was after they had met Dale Roberston, obtained an autographed picture, and taken the "Chance."

So, we built the town, and in the center of the corral, we had negotiated to have the famous Gilley's mechanical bull for the world to see and try to ride. We ran ads in all the oil field trade journals with Dale Robertson's picture, challenging visitors to come *Take the Chance*. If a visitor tried to ride the bull, he or she would get a cool button to wear around the show saying *I took the Chance*. The only ones wearing those buttons had actually been on the bull. Maybe they got tossed—most did—or maybe they didn't. Nonetheless, they had the tenacity to get on it, which created a vibrant testosterone discussion of courage that echoed throughout the conference for four days. We were definitely the show studs that year and, of financial note, sold $8 million worth of spiral weight drill pipe in four days out of a booth where we were not supposed to sell product. Needless to say, it was a stellar product and, more importantly, brand launch.

To complete the brand alignment initiative following our successful start, the Chance name became the focal point of everything we strategized and produced. Whether it was the building signage, product catalogs, industry trade journal ads, plant tours, promotional items, proposals, presentations, truck graphics, customer entertainment events, or even the labels on the actual drill pipe, everything aligned with Chance. What once was a drill pipe company without direction became a well-aligned machine.

Chance Collar Company Today

The brand took off, and Chance Collar Company rode the wave of excitement from the launch for a few years. They experienced record growth and were soon acquired by W. R. Grace. The leadership team made an awful lot of money and continued to work in the industry for a time before retiring. Glenn G. Chance passed away in 2016, at 86 years of age, with a loving family around him. The man was always full of life and loved putting life in others. He gave me my chance when he, Jim, and Dick invested in a 24-year-old kid—for which I am forever grateful.

POTHOLES HIT: 1

INTERNAL MARKETING EMPLOYEES

Brand OFF! The internal marketing team was so focused on tactical initiatives that they had not seen the big opportunity right in front of them the whole time: the name Chance. As in many instances, internal marketing was busy chasing what we like to call *shiny new objects* in their marketing tool chest. When an internal team gets busy with day-to-day, industry-trending tactics, it is really easy for them not to see the bigger opportunities. Everything they were creating and producing had a different look and feel and did not align with the organization. Everyone was kind of doing their own thing, and there was not a cohesive direction.

Brand ON! Fortunately, we got the opportunity and made the most of it by taking the chance.

POWER UP! THE POINT OF ALIGNMENT

Intentionally capitalize on the unique name Chance

CHAPTER 5

Is Your Brand in Alignment?

You just read six success stories about the leaders of smaller organizations across different industries whose enterprises had misalignments to varying degrees. Ultimately, they uncovered and embraced their hidden opportunities and realigned their brands for exponential success. Do you see yourself in any of these stories? Do you relate to any of the hidden potholes they hit along the way? How are you supposed to determine if your brand is in alignment?

Following are the steps you should take and questions you need to answer to begin your self-assessment. As you progress through them, you will begin noticing where your brand is on or off. Once you complete this assessment, you will see a much clearer picture of your brand and have a strong sense of what needs to be done to bring it into alignment if it is not already. Should you have the resources, available talent, or counsel to broaden the scope of your evaluation beyond yourself, this powerful assessment will most certainly help you prepare for the journey.

STEP 1: THE BRAINDRAIN

The truth is, you inherently know if your brand is in alignment or not. Just to make sure, let's look at the best way to begin your own assessment, which is with the proprietary, deep-dive alignment tool I call *The BrainDrain*. You can access this and other free tools at www .brandoncolemanjr.com.

You inherently know if your brand is in alignment or not.

After selling my first brand consultancy and ad agency, I started an independent consulting firm named Big Picture Thinking to lead creative think tanks around the country and work on select brand alignment projects as they presented themselves. Prior to launching the firm, I studied my notes from years in the business of helping clients with their brand strategies and alignment execution. One of my observations was our consistent use of a collection of in-depth questions, tailored to different industries, which we used to initiate every project. I captured all of those questions and refined them into *The BrainDrain*, which I have kept current throughout the years. AI is going to love it!

As an act of gratitude, I have made this document available at no charge to all *Brand ON!* readers. It includes 200 questions we have to answer as business owners and leaders if we are going to bring our brands into alignment. They are the exact same commonsense questions I ask on the front end of every engagement. They are not physically included in the back of this book only because you would jump straight to them before you finish reading the entire work. *The BrainDrain* is available to you online at any time. I recommend finishing the book before you try to answer the questions, because we wouldn't want you getting the cart before the horse. We don't do that in Texas, nor take kindly to those who do.

STEP 2: THE BRAND ALIGNMENT CHECKLIST

The Brand Alignment Checklist is another tool that can be downloaded from www.brandoncolemanjr.com at any time. It includes over 100 brand alignment points most businesses experience. It is intended to be a simple awareness inventory of your brand. Don't overthink this exercise as your gut instinct will reveal the honest answers.

Quickly review each item relevant to your situation, and check whether you believe it is Brand ON! or Brand OFF! For example, take the line item "Entity Name." Is your current name right for your business, or have you been thinking it is holding you back? Tip: If you can't immediately check a line item as Brand ON!, then it is probably Brand OFF! Remember, it either makes immediate sense, or it doesn't. Once you have all your answers to The BrainDrain and the Brand Alignment Checklist, it is time to take a walkthrough.

STEP 3: THE WALKTHROUGH

When was the last time you physically walked through your customer's journey from start to finish? I am not asking about the last time you sat in a boardroom or back office and discussed it or when your marketing person walked it for you. When was the last time you physically walked it—or drove it or clicked it or whatever is relevant to your organization's customers, patients, or donors. If you don't readily remember, it's been far too long. If you have never done it, shame on you. If you are about to start a new business, please complete a virtual walkthrough before you finalize your start-up plans.

⚡

When was the last time you physically walked through your customer's journey from start to finish?

You have to be diligent in your walk to be sure you are seeing things from your prospects' and customers' view throughout the entire journey. If you don't think you can walk it with unbiased eyes, hire someone you trust to walk it with you, and pay close attention to their remarks. Make a comprehensive list of everyone's observations. Hire some customers to walk it with you. Customers aren't always right, but they are customers. Walk through it and identify where you are Brand ON! and where you are Brand OFF! This form of what I call *physical immersion research* is critical to your assessment success. I never start a project without it.

When you engage in your customer journey walkthrough, pay special attention to your OMS. While the term *order management system* may mean slightly different things to different people, we will identify it here as whatever system you are using that supports all the phases in your company's sales process, from order creation through fulfillment to returns and follow-through. For many businesses today, OMS platforms are actual software programs that provide a single, centralized system for managing orders from multiple sales channels. This might include brick-and-mortar locations, websites, call centers, mobile orders, kiosks, and more. An automated system can simplify the buying process for customers and can make it far easier to manage orders, inventory, fulfillment, and returns for your business. Automated or manual, ideally, you will review this system in tandem with the total walkthrough you need to complete.

A Sample Walkthrough

Following is a sample walkthrough of a restaurant experience from a customer's perspective. We all eat out, so it is certainly relatable. It's fairly long but is well worth the read, because it will show you how all the little things in your customer journey add up to a brand alignment that works. Some will be things you may want to consider on your own walkthrough.

Where does brand alignment begin for you with the restaurant? How did you first learn about it? Did you drive by and witness it being built? Was it mentioned in an online article announcing the highly touted chef who was leading the culinary charge, a five-star post on social, or did someone eat there and personally tell you about their great experience? You decided to go. Was it a convenient location? Was the signage impressive? How was the parking experience? Did the approach to the building have a welcoming pedestrian feel? How did the overall physical facade of the building feel as you walked up to the front doors? Once inside, think about your greeting experience. Was the host or hostess prompt, friendly, and attentive, or did they have the attitude that you were lucky to be eating with them? How did the place smell? Did it confirm you were in a good spot or make you want to head back to the car?

Now think of your table. Did it make you feel special or just like one of the herd? Was it a quality chair or booth that gave you comfort, or were you already thinking about when you could leave? Was the background music pleasing and appropriate with the brand, or were you in a sushi house hearing country and western music? Did the crowd—or the lack thereof—appear to be people you want to dine with? Was the noise level appropriate with the style of place you were dining in? How was the overall table setting? Were the water glasses crystal clean, or did you see soap marks dotting the glass or, worse yet, lipstick?

How long was it before you were greeted by a server, and how was that overall experience? In today's climate, even the best restaurants are struggling to hire talented people in those roles who care about serving others. Did the server get you excited about the menu offerings, or was it more like a "Here's the menu, and I'll be back later" kind of thing? How did the menu look and feel, before you even started reviewing your ordering options? Was it in alignment with your expectation of the brand to that point? Did the food options exceed or at least meet what you had anticipated? Did anything excite you about the menu, or was it more of the same ol' thing? Could you tell by the menu what food made the restaurant great? Was anything obviously missing from the offering? Like, were you at a fancy new Mexican restaurant that didn't offer enchiladas? Were there any offerings that were absolutely out of whack with the brand and made you hesitate in a doubtful kind of way? Did anything they offer feel Brand OFF?

All of those questions, and we haven't even taken a bite yet! Stay on point here as we continue to review the restaurant's brand alignment. Did you feel confident that the server understood your order and that the food was going to come out right? What was happening at the table, if anything, while you waited for your order? Was there something to nibble on to keep the process flowing? If you had to go to the restroom, how was that experience? How long did it take the food to come out of the kitchen to the table? Was it an appropriate wait time? How was it presented to the table, and did they serve the right thing to the right person, or did they send a busboy over to deliver the meal who didn't have a clue? Was the food plated with a design and arrangement flair or just sitting there looking lifeless? Did the food appear hot and fresh? Did the food visually excite your senses? How was that first bite? Did it set the tone for the meal or, based on your experience so far, reset the tone for the meal? Was the food flavorful, and did it exceed your expectations? Were your additional needs, drink refills, condiments, etc., all delivered in a timely manner throughout your meal?

And how about when it was time to leave? Were they prompt with the check, or did you have to send out a search party for your server? Could you read the check? Quick note: Most food checks are printed in such tiny type they are frustrating to try to read, even with glasses. Some restaurants are learning this upsets people at the end of their experience, so they are now presenting in a way that is easier on your eyes. This would make sense, since the largest and wealthiest segment of diners at this time are from the baby boomer generation. Did the server or a manager collect your credit card in prompt fashion, or did you have to wave it up in the air over your head? Had they cleared most or all of the dirty dishes from the table by now? Did they bring your check back with a spirit of gratitude?

As you exited the restaurant, were you appreciated again as you left the front door? Did you walk to your car or Uber with a feeling the restaurant had met or exceeded your expectations? Did you look forward to telling others about your experience and returning soon? Did the restaurant touch all of your senses—visual (sight), auditory (sound), olfactory (smell), gustation (taste), and tactile (touch)? In essence, did it all make sense? Was the brand's alignment easy to assimilate? Did you get it, or was it not gettable? What is now in your one mind space for that restaurant?

Daunting isn't it? Imagine leading a restaurant or even, far more challenging, a chain of restaurants to deliver the perfect brand alignment day in and day out. And I didn't even get into all of the social, marketing, or advertising campaigns and subtleties that go along with that customer journey. It's a massive undertaking and responsibility. It is why, as a consumer, you learn to lower your expectations for some eateries and take great joy in frequenting those very few who do get it right.

Can you identify where you are Brand ON! and Brand OFF?

Now how does this all work for your brand? Can you identify where you are Brand ON! and Brand OFF? Like the restaurant, there are multiple facets to a properly aligned brand, and they vary wildly by industry. Regardless of your industry or size of your business, you have a customer journey that needs your attention. Remember, brand alignment occurs when the customer experience meets customer expectations, while achieving Brand ON! is a step beyond that. And the journey never ends.

STEP 4: COMPLETING YOUR ASSESSMENT

In addition to completing The BrainDrain, the Brand Alignment Checklist, and the list of observations you compiled in your walk-through, what are the other items you have had on your mind for quite some time? What are the things you know aren't right? Are there any hidden opportunities? As I mentioned earlier, you inherently know if your brand is in alignment or not. If anything is telling you it is not, then it is not. Make sure you add all of those items to your list.

Have you identified your point of alignment? Do you know what your one thing is? If you aren't certain, ask. Talk about it with customers, friends, and family. Go through it all with your team. If there is any confusion or disagreement, get a pro in there to give you honest and direct feedback, even if you don't want to hear it. If you do bring in outside counsel, I propose your biggest challenge will be not wanting to—or being able to—hear it. That's because, much of the time, the opportunity is not what the leader thinks it is.

My intent with this chapter is to provide you the landscape I have personally watched unfold in thousands of project engagements with countless successful entrepreneurs and top executives. I have seen all of the potholes, so if I can prevent just one reader from making a mistake or can help you find that one hidden opportunity, this effort was totally worth it. That is why I am providing you access to the commonsense questions in The BrainDrain and the Brand Alignment Checklist. I really want to encourage you to take an exhaustive look at your brand.

I keep mentioning common sense because, if your brand doesn't make immediate common sense, then it doesn't make sense at all. If you can't deliver a compelling presentation of what makes your company great in a short elevator ride, then you are doomed to creating more confusion than results. If you can't fill that one mind space with a meaningful and lasting message, then you may have a business, but you don't have a brand. There is a reason X (formerly Twitter) only allows 280 characters. It's because it is more than enough room to communicate your point on that platform. You should be able to provide a compelling brand case in the same amount of space.

It continues to amaze me how many organizations will pay a million-plus dollars for giant management consultancies to provide them ground cover via overly large presentation decks chock-full of process to optimize their brand. I have yet to see one that can be presented on that elevator ride. Don't get me wrong; I have seen some very well-done presentations and have even created a few of these immense documents myself, but in the end, it must all be very simple. Ironically, you can usually scroll through those monstrosities and find the one page that has the *one thing*. That one page with the *one thing* is all you really need to know to maximize the power of your brand.

What is your *one thing*? No, I am not beating a dead horse. We don't do that in Texas either. I am hoping to drill into my readers the one thing I would impress upon you if you were paying me to personally be in your office leading your brand alignment project: Keep it simple. It is much harder for me to convince you in a book than it would be if I were standing in front of you jumping up and down emphatically telling you to keep it simple, then turning around and showing you how.

Keep it simple.

Do you know the most common feedback I get from owners, entrepreneurs, and C-level leaders after we help them identify and realign their brand? It usually goes just like this: "Damn, that was easy. It's so obvious and simple." Months later, after implementation, it is always followed by "What a positive impact this has had on our company. People love it!"

Brand ON!

Keeping it simple is actually the hardest thing to do, or you would have already done so. Finding that one thing requires the utmost in clarity. It demands honest and sometimes painful assessment. Setting aside your pride is essential. Have you determined whether your brand is in alignment? Don't you already know?

CHAPTER 6

Aligning Your Brand

By now you are probably asking, "How do I align my brand and keep my car out of the potholes? How do I pull off a Buc-ee's, Tony Chachere's, SafeWay Driving, Santa's Wonderland, Chance Collar Company, Doctors Implants, or The Association type story? My business is nothing like those businesses, but I want to experience both the immediate and long-term success they have accomplished." Guess what? They thought the same thing at some point in time. However, once they found the hidden power of brand alignment for their organizations, they knew they were onto something big. I have yet to meet a business or organization that can't be aligned.

While no book or consultant could ever provide you an absolute alignment strategy for your unique brand without a thorough review of your total situation, I am confident once you complete the assessment process we discussed earlier, you will be well on your way to determining your best approach and strategies for the future.

— ⚡ —

I have yet to meet a business or organization that can't be aligned.

However, before you jump in to begin aligning everything, let's look at a few key discoveries I have made throughout my journey that I believe will be helpful to you. Think about these five considerations and what role they may be able to play in the future of your enterprise. Perhaps they will help you identify your point of alignment or improve the core values that will drive your brand. They are purposeful strategic thought areas I have not seen change in five decades.

YOUR BRAND'S ATMOSPHERE

Let's return to the dating analogy I used earlier in the book. Think back to a date night where you created the perfect atmosphere. You made sure everything was just right. Remember the music, lights, wine, dinner, attire, grooming, aromas, room temperature, and how it all felt? You instinctively were trying to affect all of the human senses to influence the environment: visual (sight), auditory (sound), olfactory (smell), gustation (taste), and tactile (touch). You went to great lengths to ensure you put your best foot forward. It generated internal excitement and provided you a magical sense of confidence.

The stage was perfectly set to have a positive experience. In a sense, by creating the right atmosphere, you had successfully created brand alignment for your personal brand.

Pause for a moment and consider the atmosphere of your brand. How does your brand's atmosphere affect the human senses? Think of your specific customer journey and all of those customer touchpoints. How are they affecting the response of your intended target? Are they in sync? Have they set a pervading tone or mood around your brand that compels the customer response you desire? Do they create the environment to set the stage for success? Do they fulfill the desired mind space? Is your CX set up to succeed?

That's an oversimplification, maybe. Maybe not. How different is setting the atmosphere for your date night and setting the atmosphere for your brand? In both cases, you are establishing the environment for success, regardless of your product or service offering. In both cases, anything out of alignment can destroy the potential outcome. If you will consider the atmosphere around your brand and how everything revolves around it, it may provide you the clarity you need to bring it into alignment.

As you are well aware, technology plays a major role in your customer experience model, which affects your brand's atmosphere on a daily basis. If you have someone on your team in charge of commerce, make certain they are proactively managing your customer relationship management system. If you run a sole proprietorship, then you need to make sure you are focused on the discipline of customer relationships. This comes naturally to some hard-charging entrepreneurs but not so much to others. Either way, all of your management and outreach technologies have to be in alignment to produce the frictionless messaging and interaction today's customers are seeking.

How does your brand's atmosphere affect the human senses?

Creating your brand's atmosphere is no different from getting ready for that special date you had once upon a time. You went to the effort to make sure everything was in perfect alignment. Doing the same for your brand will provide you clarity unlike anything you have ever experienced. When you succeed at creating that perfect atmosphere, you will have succeeded at bringing your brand into alignment.

FINDING THAT ONE THING

Much is written about finding the one thing in many different facets of your personal life, whether it be God's purpose for your life, the one thing you are supposed to focus on today, the one thing you want to do before you die, and so on. There are a plethora of books, workshops, seminars, and other resources available to help you narrow your focus and find those personal one things.

As you know by now, the *one thing* I am talking about in this book is totally related to your brand and its point of alignment, for which there is very little information published. This one thing is all about properly filling that one mind space your stakeholders allow for your brand. For illustration purposes and, hopefully, to help you identify your one thing, I have created the following list of some major brands and their one thing. Each of these big brands has a vast array of product and service offerings, but you will notice they still only get one mind space from which to leverage their brand:

BRAND	ONE THING
Wrangler	Jeans
Michelin	Tires
Subway	Sandwich
FedEx	Overnight
McKinsey	Consulting
Cole Haan	Shoes
Nationwide	Insurance
Deloitte	Accounting
Chanel	Perfume

I used national brands as examples so most of you will be able to associate with them. However, the same theory works for small online and neighborhood businesses as well. You do not have to invest millions of dollars to become a well-aligned and known brand at the local level, but you do need to be aware of bringing your brand into alignment. You may or may not become known by millions, but chances are, you don't need to be known by the masses to be successful, just by your neighborhood or your followers. Most importantly, you need to be very well-known—and loved—by your target constituency. You need to fill their one mind space with your point of alignment.

This is a good spot to talk briefly about naming a product or entity. If you will notice, not a single one of the brand names in the aforementioned list tells you what the product or company is about. Each of those entities started from scratch and built their brand over time. The point is, your name does not have to say specifically what you do, as is evidenced by the recent onslaught of really weird names that are making a killing online. One of the reasons this has occurred is that many of the great names that do actually convey what a specific brand is about are already taken, so it gets harder over time to own one. It is an added advantage if you can include what you do in your name, but it is certainly not necessary.

_____ ⚡ _____

Your name does not have to say specifically what you do.

_____

We have created a significant number of brand names and would like to share some very basic tips for selecting one. It is smart to make sure the word or words are easy to say and spell. It is also best if it flows well off the tongue. It needs to be memorable and not so unique that people can't remember it. The shorter, the better, as long as it works. Don't pick a name that is so close to a well-known name that it will make someone think of the known name instead of yours. And make sure it is also internet friendly, so the search engines will love you. These are very basic tips; a lot goes into creating the best name for your venture. Every now and then, a great pick for your name just jumps out, and it works. If that has happened to you, congrats. If you are about to select a name or rename your company or product, take the time to get it right. If you think you need professional help, get it from a proven source; there is so much to consider to make it the powerful asset it should be. Moreover, the wrong name will be a constant albatross.

Your name is but one consideration in your overall brand alignment. What else sticks with people about your brand? You probably already know what your one thing is, that one point of alignment. Many times, that one thing actually compels someone to start a business or launch a product in the first place. If you don't know what it is, chances are you will discover it when you complete the process outlined in the previous chapter. If not, then you have more work to do, because it is critically important you precisely fill that one mind space to maximize your potential. It is the only way to capture the power of an aligned brand. Like Curly said, "If your brand is not in alignment, nothing else means shit." Well, that might not have been Curly.

YOUR SECOND MOST VALUABLE ASSET

I will always believe your most valuable asset is your aligned brand, because it provides the promise and delivery needed to attract and keep customers. The second most valuable asset you have is your existing customers. The single most frequent mistake I have observed in 50 years is companies taking their existing customer, client, patient, or donor base for granted. When you do so, it is without a doubt the largest line item on the liability ledger.

The cost of developing new business is one of the highest costs most companies have. Your acquisition costs consist of all sales, marketing, and advertising expenses plus, in many cases, your people's time and talents as well. Regardless of the type of business you own, you have to make sure your customer acquisition costs do not exceed the lifetime value of your customer, or LVC. In fact, current consulting wisdom suggests your CAC (customer acquisition cost) should not exceed one-third of your LVC. This varies by industry, but you get the point: Customers already buying from you are extremely valuable, so you should never take them for granted.

The owner of a small catering business I frequently used had experienced solid growth over 10 years and built a customer base of approximately 200 loyal regulars. Things were rocking for this entrepreneur, and he could do no wrong, so he began expanding into other areas. Like any small business, the ever-perplexing 80/20 theory was in play, and 20% of his customers were generating 80% of his annual sales. As usually happens, over time, competition creeped in, along with changes in leadership at a few of his top 20% customers, and all of a sudden, he found himself losing a lot of business and financially upside down.

His immediate reaction was to put more money into advertising. His business is located in a smaller market, so TV, radio, and billboards were not overly expensive. He loaded up on his media spend and really started pushing his business. It was not working, so he spent more money changing the creative and the messaging. It did not move the needle either. Nothing he tried was working, so he reached out to me for help.

We had helped him over a decade earlier by totally realigning his brand, so I knew he had a solid baseline for success. I sat down with him and listened to his story for over an hour. He was visibly shaken. Sales had dropped 70%, and he had increased expenditures beyond reason in an attempt to resuscitate his market. It was easy to see the personal pressure was taking a physical toll, and I hurt for him.

Once he was finished, I asked him only one question: "When was the last time you thanked your customers?"

He looked at me like, *Hey man, I just poured out all my business and life challenges and you have the balls to ask me when is the last time I thanked my customers?* From his eyes I read, *I always thank my customers.*

Actually, he had not said a word in response to my question. He was numb and probably a bit upset with me. I repeated myself, "When was the last time you thanked your customers?"

He then verbally stated the obvious, "I have trained my staff to always say thank you when we are leaving any catering event."

I knew that would be the answer. It always is. Every business owner or leader *thinks* they thank their customers, but do they really?

I told him he was going to build his business back in three months and, by the end of the year, would be rocking at original levels plus some additional growth. He looked at me like I was smoking something and said, "How are you going to do that?"

I told him I was not going to do it; he was.

Word for word, here is what I recommended: "First, assemble a list of your customers in descending order from the biggest spender to the lowest. There will be a natural break somewhere around the top 20%, where there is a drastic falloff in annual sales volume. Draw a line there. Find a company that will print custom aprons for you and put your big logo on them." (A decade earlier, we had created a fun logo for him that captured his personality, and everyone loved it. It had actually become a well-loved icon around town.) "Buy 50 of them in white, printed with your iconic logo, then have your team gift wrap them in your company colors with a nice bow on top. You personally start at the top of your list and go see each customer. Do not tell them you are coming. Just arrive at their office, and tell the receptionist you are there to bring them a gift. When you have a wrapped gift in hand, there are very few times you will be turned away, and if you are, tell the receptionist you will come back another day, but do not leave the gift." Remember, this is a smaller city, so most everyone knows this guy.

By this time, he really thought I had lost my marbles. He was expecting something far more magical from the brand guru. I encouraged him to keep taking notes. "When you get in front of your customer, simply tell them how much you have appreciated all of their past business and that you just wanted to stop by and say thank you. They will respond with an expression of shock, followed by a big smile. At that time, shake their hand, and walk out. Do not, under any circumstance, talk business. If they say they have an event coming up that they want to talk to you about, tell them you appreciate it but you will come back to see them at a convenient time. Do not, under any circumstance, take an order. Do not lose the shock value and the genuine feeling of appreciation they will experience."

He said, "You mean, even if he or she wants to write up an order, I don't accept it?"

I said, "Correct. But it is okay to show excitement about the order. Then, set a time to come back and see them. You want to be emphatic that this visit is about appreciation, not selling."

Less than a month later, I received a call from him. He was so excited he could barely talk. He told me the response had been so overwhelming he was having trouble keeping up with the orders. He also said he got back two of his biggest customers immediately, and he knew more were to follow. He noted that the energy and spirit around his team had gone through the roof and that everyone was doing their job better. To sum it all up, he said, "We have hope again!" This pattern continued, and his business grew more than he ever imagined possible.

Consider how impactful gratitude would be if you are in the high-dollar consulting world where any single client could be worth millions to your firm. The cost of acquiring and cultivating that client is enormous, and no matter how challenging they become to serve, they are far more cost effective than the one you have to start with from the beginning. Client acquisition is expensive and resource consuming. Wouldn't you be better off spending more of those resources showing genuine appreciation to existing clients? It amazes me how many businesses use the same old methodologies of appreciation that don't really come across as genuine simply because they are so commonplace. Get creative with your genuine appreciation, and don't fall into the normal trap of taking your clients for granted. It is so much more profitable to take care of your existing clients than it is to go find new ones. Or as the cowboys would tell you, "It's much easier to catch the horse that's in the barn than the one that's running out on the open plains."

---------------- ⚡ ----------------

"It's much easier to catch the horse that's in the barn than the one that's running out on the open plains."

THE ENERGY OF GRATITUDE

Fourthly, be mindful that gratitude is not only part of a virtuous life but, in my opinion, the single most influential brand alignment strategy. Neuroscientists have proven the expression of gratitude produces chemicals in the brain—dopamine, serotonin, and oxytocin—that make people feel peaceful and happy. Robert A. Emmons, a renowned psychology professor at the University of California, is considered by many to be the world's leading scientific expert on gratitude. He and his associates have conducted numerous studies showing the relationship between gratitude and feelings of happiness. In his book, *Thanks! How the New Science of Gratitude Can Make You Happier*, Emmons suggests you intentionally integrate gratitude into your daily life, noting that it heals, energizes, and has lasting effects on your well-being.

Integrating genuine gratitude into your business will amplify the well-being of your organization as well. Moreover, making it the foundation of your brand alignment will build enduring customer relationships while driving lifelong profits. Being grateful should be at the core of your CX if you want to differentiate yourself and establish your brand as a trusted partner.

How often does your client, customer, donor, or patient base feel genuine appreciation? Printing "Thank you for your business" on an invoice doesn't even come close, nor does hanging a sign in your store saying "We appreciate our customers." Sorry, but that is all really old-school BS. Immerse yourself in your customer journey, and ask what gratitude should look like to the people who keep your business flowing. We all like to feel we are appreciated. When we begin feeling like we are being taken for granted, we make changes. What would it cost for you to replace all of your customers today? How long would it take?

Gratitude is the single most influential brand alignment strategy.

If you already live your personal life from a place of gratitude, this approach will be second nature. If you separate business from personal, then you probably don't get it, because business is personal when in alignment. I have encountered a sizable number of what I consider mediocre leaders who don't put gratitude at the forefront of their business. Most of the time, it is because they have the same issue being grateful in their personal lives, so it flows over into their business. It's really hard to fake gratitude.

Genuine gratitude drives so much positive energy that I am constantly surprised by those who choose not to embrace it in their business. It's long been known the closer you want to get to someone, the more you start expressing gratitude toward that person. That being the case, wouldn't it make sense the same would work with your stakeholder groups, from investors to customers? Why not improve the lives of all of those involved with your business by integrating the synergy and enthusiasm of gratitude into your culture and customer experience? The sooner you do, the sooner you will bring your brand into true alignment.

Finally, with the integration of so much technology and automation into our customer relationships, we need to be extremely mindful of gratitude so we don't lose touch with the human side of the buying equation. Until AI buys and sells from itself, business will continue to be personal.

YOUR PERSONAL BRAND

While the focus of this book is on company and product brands as they relate to small business, it is important to note one of the great recent developments on the branding landscape is the professional attention to personal brands. Over the past 25 years or so, our nation has watched some of the most prevalent corporate brands fail: Enron, WorldCom, Kodak, Lehman Brothers, GM, and many others. When combined with bank failures and significant mismanagement by the US government, it's no wonder our trust in large institutions has waned to an all-time low.

Because of this phenomenon, our society has shifted its trust to believing in people first and business brands a distant second. Therefore, it is incredibly important for entrepreneurs to pay close attention to their personal brands, since they are the face of most small businesses. Not only are they the face, but quite often the heartbeat, spirit, and personae that permeate the culture of the brand.

While many leaders have inherently managed their personal brands through their own lifestyle, words, and actions, that is no longer enough on our new social landscape. Many of your prospective customers, current customers, employees, and other stakeholders will be judging you and your business online long before they ever meet you in person. Therefore, you want to make sure you intentionally put your authentic, human self out front in your social media endeavors, as opposed to treating them like bothersome afterthoughts. You may even benefit from having your own personal website that implicitly supports the foundation of your company endeavors.

Don't misunderstand. The equity you build in your name, and therefore your business, is not about bragging or being self-absorbed. If you take that approach it will not serve you well. However, if your personal story is told and shared in such a way it adds trust and credibility to your enterprise, the power of your brand will significantly expand. Take the time to craft a story that is a genuine expression of what you are all about as a person. Make certain it represents your core values and is a realistic expression of what makes you unique. After all, your uniqueness is probably why you are in the business you choose to own in the first place.

A lot goes into creating and launching a personal brand. Even if you are already a special character in your own right, capturing your essence and opening up your authenticity to the world is a whole other skill set. Remember the part of this book where we talked about getting out of our own way? Even this branding guy hired someone to help me brand myself. There are a few really good personal branding firms who have climbed to the forefront of our industry, and I would recommend seeking the counsel of one if you are the face of your organization.

CHAPTER 7

Turning Your Brand ON!

I t's go time! Once you have completed the self-assessment, you should have a comprehensive list of observations and ideas derived from the questions you answered and things you observed. This immersive and exhaustive process should provide you with a clear understanding of your most profound opportunities and give you an indication where you should start developing a plan of action. Whether that is a change in your name, your business model, your product or service offering, your communications, or whatever the case may be, you will know where to begin.

CREATING AN ACTION PLAN

Your next steps depend on what you uncover while completing your assessment. I have counseled clients who only needed to change one item to bring their brand into alignment. For them, an action plan was relatively easy, and they were done in less than a week. They implemented the change, and off they went down the road to smooth driving success.

For others, it may require a wholesale initiative. For whatever myriads of reasons, all four of their wheels are shot, the rims are bent, and the tires are about to blow. Depending on your business situation, you may have to pivot or bring in outside help to pull it all together. This type of initiative could last anywhere from 9 to 18 months. The pandemic created this situation for a lot of businesses, and it obviously commands a more complex plan of action.

If you are like most people, you will probably fall somewhere in the middle and have a very manageable project ahead that may take you three to six months to complete. Either way, the best piece of advice I can give you is to get started now. Remember that every day your car is out of alignment is another day of a rough ride, so why wait? The tires only get worse. In all my years, I never had a client tell me they wish they had waited longer to get started. In fact, it is usually quite the opposite. "Why didn't we do this sooner?"

Fast-forward: You have identified your hidden opportunities and triumphantly aligned—or realigned—your brand. You and your team have successfully launched a comprehensive strategy, and all of the initial feedback is encouraging. You are confident in the brand alignment you have created. You are happy you initiated this project and know it is going to create positive short and long-term success for your business. You are and should be anticipating great things to come.

WHAT TO EXPECT

Great things will happen once you have aligned your brand for success. Done right, you should anticipate a more natural flow in your business, an inspired workforce, increased sales, and a more engaged customer base. Referrals should increase while complaints decrease. Your full range of stakeholders will feel the buzz that alignment creates. You will experience a better return on your social and advertising spends. Your message retention and brand awareness should go up, and customer loyalty ought to go through the roof. The entire culture around your organization will compel team members to engage with your brand on a more meaningful level. At the end of the day, everyone will feel better about your business except your competitors.

You also need to prepare for the warning signs I guarantee will occur down the road. As sure as you are reading this page, others will try to change what you have done. Keep the Top 7 Potholes on your smartphone and review it once a month. Stop any and all movements by anyone, including yourself, from steering toward those potholes. Be keenly aware of internal or external influencers who want to put their mark on something. Know whether it is one month, one year, or three years down the road, there will be recommendations and pleas for change in one form or another. The one commonality of all of the success stories I shared with you is that every single one of those clients has shown relentless discipline in the consistent execution of their brand.

— ⚡ —

Every single one of those clients has shown relentless discipline in the consistent execution of their brand.

Remember the power of the great brands that last 25 years or longer. Be aware that, even though you and your team see your brand daily, your customers don't. They have one mind space for your brand and are only thinking of you on occasion. They don't get tired of your brand outreach nearly as quickly as you and your team do. In fact, I have noticed through the years on most ad campaigns and branding initiatives that the internal team gets tired of the messaging just about the time the outreach is starting to achieve its potential. I cannot even begin to estimate the amount of money and resources I have seen wasted by changing campaigns too quickly.

Consistency, when your brand is out of alignment, is not a good thing. However, consistency, once you have brand alignment, is extremely powerful. That doesn't mean you won't make adjustments along the way because you will, but they will not be major unless your brand alignment project was a failure. There will be tweaks and improvements. Be mindful your brand has certain aspects of fluidity and the customer journey never ends. But it does have a starting point and a multitude of touchpoints that are in your control. The key is to remain mindful of your brand's alignment and make sure your team is on board. The key is discipline.

—————————— ⚡ ——————————

Consistency, once you have brand alignment, is extremely powerful.

Externally, that means staying in touch with your customers' shifting needs, mindsets, and preferences throughout that journey. That encompasses setting the right expectations at the right time. It requires you to drive continual engagement and to ensure your brand's personality is fun and inspirational. It means you are accountable and transparent to your customers, always communicating *with* them and not *at* them.

Internally, with your brand in alignment, your team of employees should all be engaged and excited about the future of the brand. If they are not, they will be your biggest hurdle in a sustained execution. If you own a small coffee shop, those baristas need to embody the spirit of the atmosphere. If you have a larger business, it could be a partner, investor, admin, or marketing person who poisons the well with a bad attitude. Don't take this scenario lightly, because that cancer needs to be cured or excised before it spreads. The cost for not doing so is too great not to make it a priority. If you are going to have a winning brand alignment, your team needs to believe in it and be prepared to sustain it. Witness the simple power of Chick-fil-A's approach to naming their employees Team Members and instilling in them the value of responding to all customer *thank you*s with "My pleasure," which is an endearing, emphatic, and polite response. It is the small things that will make a difference in your brand alignment.

--- ⚡ ---

Don't allow a team member to poison the well with a bad attitude.

Be mindful of these warning signs, and address them as soon as they surface. We are all aware of scope creep on a project. Brand creep is very similar. All of the various inputs you receive from different sources will tend to morph the brand if you allow it. A small project here or a website change there, and before you know it, you are Brand OFF!

BRAND ALIGNMENT IN THE FUTURE

There is no need to tell you the world we are operating in is vastly different from what it was just a few years ago. Most everything is changing in one way or another, and I don't pretend to know the precise future of brand alignment. What I can state for certain is that the principles I have shared with you have not changed in 50 years. I also believe that, as long as there are humans involved in the buying and selling process, there will be a strong need for brand alignment. That being said, let's explore two major considerations that will probably impact your brand: global events and technology. While both are viewed by many as disruptors for many obvious reasons, I would like to suggest they be viewed as accelerators and opportunities for growth.

Global events

I would be remiss not to start with the COVID-19 pandemic. We are all aware of the massive impact it had on everything business, and therefore, everything brand. Chances are, you had to make some brand alignment adjustments to go along with the business changes you implemented to survive—or flourish—during that difficult time. The post-pandemic consumer wants organizations to align with their values more than ever, which, in turn, has marketing working harder to understand their customers on a deeper, more personal level.

Americus Reed II, a self-described "brand identity theorist," is a prominent marketing professor in the Wharton School, at the University of Pennsylvania. His primary research and consulting areas are in brand equity and identity loyalty. He focuses on the study of creating and fostering brand communities that transcend the utilitarian aspects of products to actualize iconic levels of symbolic identity and self-expression. He encourages brands to connect to deeper levels of emotional and social affiliation and to cultivate lifelong relationships with intermediate customers and end consumers.

In "Building Your Brand in a Post-Pandemic Market," an article for *Knowledge at Wharton* from 2023, Reed shares with author Angie Basiouny, "Consumers are in this state of heightened self-awareness about what's really important to them, so we're seeing a lot of brands really lean into the notion of a meaning system: Why do I exist? How am I making the planet better?" he said. "Broader kinds of questions that are built into the brand's DNA are rising to the surface because consumers care about that."[5]

---

5 Americus Reed, "Building Your Brand in a Post-Pandemic Market," Knowledge at Wharton, November 14, 2023, https://knowledge.wharton.upenn.edu/article/building-your-brand-in-a-post-pandemic-market/

The sociological change brought about by the pandemic will continue to have a profound impact on the way you must align with your constituencies. Earlier, we discussed the need for understanding your market in order to more effectively align perception with reality. Knowing that market well will require a deep dive into their values to better understand where they are personally and how you can connect on a meaningful level throughout their journey with you.

Who knows when or how another global issue will impact the future of business. It is important to remain mindful of your brand as you navigate the next major shift we will most certainly experience at some point.

Technology

Considering the high speed at which technology is changing everything, I must address the entry of AI into the brand alignment landscape. While most in marketing appreciate AI's contribution to increasing speed and productivity, many agree that that the creative applications of AI are trailing behind. Yet the applications of AI in marketing will continue to evolve. To illustrate that point, I will share information I have gleaned from two of my favorite go-to sources, both of which I have read since the first day of my career: *Ad Age* and the *McKinsey Quarterly*.

A recent white paper in *Ad Age*, "How AI Is Taking Marketing Efficiency to the Next Level," quotes Carola Leiva, a senior product manager of Klaviyo, an intelligent marketing automation company, who does a good job of summarizing the future of AI in our industry:

Once you start to really power these large language models with information about what works for your customers, then you can potentially not only have a creative message, but one that we can predict how it's going to work for your specific recipients—meaning we won't even need to send it out to know how it's going to perform.[6]

When I read this white paper and look back at the different branding and marketing initiatives I have encountered, it is easy for me to see the massive opportunities for AI to improve the development and activation process far beyond anything ever imagined. The speed, efficiency, and consistency alone will significantly shorten the brand development cycle and reduce work redundancy. Its efficiencies will ultimately yield a far superior data foundation from which to create great brand work and provide more time to be humanly creative. While none of this book was written by an AI tool, that will probably not be the case in the future!

In McKinsey and Company's informative publication, *McKinsey Quarterly*, consultants specializing in generative AI also lay out examples of how the high-speed, cognitive tool will potentially benefit marketing.[7] It discusses how generative AI "has taken hold

---

6 "How AI Is Taking Marketing Efficiency to the Next Level," *Ad Age* (December 12, 2023), https://adage.com/white-paper/how-ai-taking-marketing-efficiency-next-level.

7 Michael Chui, Eric Hazan, Roger Roberts, Alex Singla, Kate Smaje, Alex Sukharevsky, Lareina Yee, and Rodney Zemmel, "The Economic Potential of Generative AI: The Next Productivity Frontier," *McKinsey Quarterly* (June 14, 2023), https://www.mckinsey.com/capabilities/mckinsey-digital/our-insights/the-economic-potential-of-generative-ai-the-next-productivity-frontier.

rapidly in marketing and sales functions, in which text-based communications and personalization at scale are driving forces. The technology can create personalized messages tailored to individual customer interests, preferences, and behaviors, as well as do tasks such as producing first drafts of brand advertising, headlines, slogans, social media posts, and product descriptions."

The article outlines how generative AI can, "significantly reduce the time required for ideation and content drafting, saving valuable time and effort." It goes on to mention how, "It can also facilitate consistency across different pieces of content, ensuring a uniform brand voice, writing style, and format." Furthermore, it discusses enhanced use of customer data, SEO optimization, and product discovery. It estimates generative AI could increase the productivity of the marketing function between 5% and 15% of the total marketing spend. I would suggest it will be closer to 20%–30% of the spend when it is all said and done.

With your newfound awareness, I am certain you will see how this disruptive technology can be a huge benefit to you and your brand in the future. Keep in mind that AI is a tool for you to use judiciously within your brand to bring it into alignment and to be consistent in its delivery. But remember, AI is based on data it already has and doesn't even really know what it is saying—at least not yet—and it is certainly not creative in the purest sense of the word.

David Ogilvy, considered the Father of Advertising, provided great insight into the creative process and how hyper logical thinking is quite often at odds with generating groundbreaking creative ideas. Long before technology, he wrote in *Confessions of an Advertising*

Man, "The creative process requires more than reason . . . Most original thinking isn't even verbal. It requires 'a groping experimentation with ideas, governed by intuitive hunches and inspired by the unconscious.' The majority of businessmen are incapable of original thinking because they are unable to escape from the tyranny of reason. Their imaginations are blocked." I am not quite sure what Mr. Ogilvy would have thought about AI in the creative process, but I do believe his observations will become even more relevant as we integrate AI into our business and marketing thinking.

There will most certainly be additional considerations that will impact brand alignment in the future. Additional societal disruption, environmental change, advancing healthcare, global finance, and there is already discussion about artificial general intelligence, which will reportedly dwarf what we are experiencing with our current AI. Whew! That's a lot to stay on top of.

READY TO TURN YOUR BRAND ON!?

Have you completed your assessment? Do you know what your one thing is? Do you have the right brand alignment mindset? Do you have systems in place to handle the growth you will experience? Is your team on board? Have you thought about the opportunities this will create to expand your business or add new product offerings? Is there a possibility or is it a goal that your brand alignment could set you up for an acquisition soon? We have aligned many brands for companies who were acquired within a few years of realignment. Is your timing right?

---- ⚡ ----

Do you have the right brand alignment mindset?

There is a reason select few organizations are in perfect alignment and achieve Brand ON! acclaim. It is only for those who understand it and are committed to being truly exceptional. It is only a simple process for those who have a deep desire to excel. Some people can't find their point of alignment or see the one thing, so they make it far more complicated than it needs to be. They inherently don't understand brand alignment. It's just not in their wheelhouse. For them, operating at 70%–80% of potential is fine. They may or may not meet customer expectations, and they will never exceed them.

Brand alignment is a delicate balance of art and science, but more importantly, it is an act of common sense. It intentionally turns the entire customer journey into your aligned brand. It is a vision with a touch. When in perfect alignment, it becomes obvious to everyone and clears the way for increased sales, brand loyalty, and higher profits. It establishes an atmosphere of success that breeds more success. It creates a winning attitude that prevails in everything you do. It becomes *Brand ON!*

I wrote this book because I have seen brand alignment change lives by advancing personal dreams through business improvement. I trust it will do the same for you when you turn your *Brand ON!*

I spent my first 50 years in business leveraging the power of aligned brands. I plan on spending the next 50 years honoring those who have achieved it!

We are in constant search of those rare entrepreneurial enterprises who have achieved perfect brand alignment. If you would like to nominate a brand to be recognized as Brand ON!, please see the nomination information in appendix B or go to www.brandoncolemanjr.com/brand-on/#nomination.

Brand Alignment FAQs

Does achieving brand alignment make it easier to run my business?

Absolutely. When strategies, ideas, hires, marketing spends, expansion, communications, or purchases come up, good decisions are much easier to make. If it doesn't align with the brand, it's an easy and resounding NO! It saves a ton of time, frustration, and resources for you and your team.

Is brand alignment a healthy pursuit of perfection?

As it relates to your brand, yes. We all know the personal pursuit of perfection can be fueled by unrealistic expectations that lead to unintended consequences, so you have to keep it in check. It's the same in your business. Striving for absolute perfection across the board can put too much pressure on you and your team and can result in fear of failure and create a cycle of doubt. However, when it comes to your brand, go for it! There is nothing wrong with the pursuit of perfection in your brand if you keep it real, and achieving it is magical.

How do I know to what degree my business is out of brand alignment?

Start with your gut. What does it tell you? I find that most leaders have a discerning instinct when their organization is out of brand alignment. Many times, you will know specifically—or, at least, think you know—exactly what feels out of alignment. Sometimes, you will point out X, but it is really Y. Next, study your customers, clients, or patients. Are their interactions with your brand crystal clear up and down the spectrum? Do you or your team feel a natural joy through-out your interactions with your customers? What are your customers saying about you in person or on social media? Are they genuine with their feedback? Do all of their purchase patterns make sense, or do you feel like you are leaving some on the table? Does your brand aura feel right? Have you asked your former customers?

How much of an investment will I need to get into brand alignment?

It depends on several factors, beginning with what type of business you have and how out of alignment you are. For some, it may be the slight tweaking of one or two customer-facing aspects of your company which will not cost very much at all. For others, it is a total overhaul, which may require a significant investment. Either way, I have never seen it not pay off in spades if done correctly, and that goes for any size organization.

How long does brand alignment take?

Depending on the complexity, it could be from one day to over a year.

When is the best time to start evaluating my brand alignment?

Now. And if your car is out of alignment, get that done ASAP as well!

Is alignment relevant in other areas of my business?

Yes. While I advocate brand alignment is paramount and sets the tone for everything relating to the customer journey, other areas of alignment can play an important role in profitability. Business process, production, finance, human resources, and technology are just a few disciplines that can show vast improvement. The more in total alignment your business is, the smoother it runs. We have seen a lot of businesses experience alignment in other areas of their organization as a by-product of their brand alignment initiative. It makes common sense.

Why is brand alignment relevant in my personal life?

Entrepreneurs' personal lives flow directly into their businesses and vice versa. There is no such thing as my personal life and my business life. They are naturally intertwined and no matter how hard you try to separate them, they impact each other. You are the face of your business, so your character and integrity matter. And now that society has shifted its trust to believing in people first and business brands second, it is incredibly important for entrepreneurs to pay close attention to their personal brands and how they choose to live their lives.

Brand ON! Acclaimed Nomination

The Brand ON! Acclaimed seal is awarded to recognize entrepreneurs whose independent brands have achieved perfect brand alignment by providing a customer experience that consistently exceeds customer expectations.

Brand ON!

We are in constant search of those rare entrepreneurial enterprises who have achieved perfect brand alignment and deserve to be recognized as Brand ON! If you would like to nominate a brand to be recognized as Brand ON!, please go to our website at www .brandoncolemanjr.com/brand-on/#nomination.

Online nominations are encouraged from any industry. Representatives of Brand ON! will review the nominations and interview finalist businesses who appear, through secondary research, to be in total brand alignment. Upon personal visitation to the business and accomplishment validation, a one-minute video will be produced featuring the business owner discussing how they achieved brand alignment and presentation of the Brand ON! Acclaimed seal of success. These videos and stories will be hosted on our website and shared across social channels to honor the recipients and inspire other small business owners.

REQUIREMENTS AND UNDERSTANDING

Businesses or nonprofits must be independently owned and operated. Franchises owned by franchisees are considered independently owned and operated businesses. Online application must be completed in its entirety. Brand ON! has full authority and final decision-making power for all selection purposes. Nominee grants Brand ON! exclusive rights to post the video and notice of the award. Brand ON! grants nominee exclusive rights to post the video and notice of the award.

Free Resources for Your Use

I hope you enjoyed reading the book and wish you the very best on your journey into brand alignment. For your *Brand ON!* bonus, scan the following QR code to get your complimentary copies of my proprietary The BrainDrain questionnaire and Brand Alignment Checklist. I personally use these tools to jump start all of my brand alignment consulting engagements.

The BrainDrain is a comprehensive list of 200 exploratory questions curated over thousands of client projects across five decades. It will serve as an excellent starting point for your brand alignment initiative and will help you begin determining whether you are Brand OFF! or Brand ON!

Brand ON!

The Brand Alignment Checklist is a master checklist of items in your business you believe to be Brand ON! or Brand OFF! Put this to work after completing The BrainDrain. Together, these resources will get you well on your way to determining what work lies ahead to be in perfect brand alignment. Should you decide to engage professional help along the way, these tools will serve as a superb beginning for your team.

GET EMPOWERED!

PODCAST

Tune in to hear *The Brand ON! Show* dropped every Tuesday. Learn the latest brand alignment insights while being entertained by Brandon's engaging style and surprise special guests.

www.brandoncolemanjr.com/empower/

THE INDEX CARD

While Brandon's minimum consulting engagement fee is $100K, it's absolutely FREE to ask any consulting question by following the link!

www.brandoncolemanjr.com/brand-on/

Index

Index

179

Index

for Doctors Implants, 94–95
general discussion, 51–53

T

target-rich environment, 89
technology, impact on alignment,
    162–165
Texas A&M alumni. *See* Aggie Network
Texas Aggie magazine, 99–103
Texas Christmas Experience, 69–73, 74
Tony Chachere's
    background of misalignment, 76
    current success, 82
    overview, 75
    potholes hit, 83
    realigning brand, 76–82
tools
    The BrainDrain questionnaire,
        128–129, 175
    Brand Alignment Checklist,
        129–130, 176
Top 7 Potholes
    Aggie Network and, 105–106
    Chance Collar Company and,
        125–126
    compromising to please others,
        54–58
    external marketing vendors, 46–48
    internal marketing employees, 43–46
    overview, 42–43
    owner's forest, 48–50
    personal pride and success, 51–53
    reviewing, 157

SafeWay Driving and, 115–116
Santa's Wonderland and, 74
Tony Chachere's and, 83
unintentional morphing, 58–59
wrong brand or concept, 53–54
tunnel vision, entrepreneurial, 48–50

U

unintentional morphing, 58–63

V

vendors, external marketing, 46–48
vision, 22–24

W

Walker, Gene, 107–116
Walker, Jeanne, 107–116
walkthrough, 130–135
Wasek, Don, 34
wrong brand or concept as pothole
    Doctors Implants, 87–88, 90–94
    general discussion, 53–54
    tips for choosing name, 144–145

WHY HE
WROTE THE BOOK.

With a legacy spanning half a century in strategic brand consulting, Brandon Coleman Jr is inspired to generously share his invaluable insights and experiences with entrepreneurs everywhere. Driven by the belief that his God-given purpose is achieving yours, Brandon has embarked on a mission of philanthropic knowledge transfer to share the incredible stories that have shaped his journey and the success of hundreds of clients. Not afraid of straight talk and willing to give away his secrets, Brandon opens up on the inside scoop in the world of marketing and branding.

About the Author

BRANDON COLEMAN JR is a renowned branding legend with the acute ability to cut through clutter to amplify others' potential. His gifted awareness and enthusiastic, all-in spirit have fueled exponential success on thousands of brand alignment engagements across many different industries spanning five decades. Brandon has the accolades and notoriety that come with launching, leading, and ultimately selling, one of the most successful mid-sized strategic branding firms in the country. He is a born visionary entrepreneur, noted speaker, author, and outstanding alumnus of Mays Business School at Texas A&M University, where he served on the dean's advisory board for twenty-five years. With a propensity for straight talk and genuine love for seeing others reach their dreams, Brandon is driven by an unselfish desire to make an immediate positive impact on your business and your life. He is a skilled storyteller who writes with a generous blend of creativity, candor, and character in a conversational manner you will find enlightening, entertaining, and inspiring.

WWW.BRANDONCOLEMANJR.COM